INTERPRETING AND UNDERSTANDING DREAMS

INTERPRETING AND UNDERSTANDING DREAMS

DAN GOLLUB

Nova Science Publishers, Inc.
Commack, New York

Editorial Production: Susan Boriotti
Office Manager: Annette Hellinger
Graphics: Frank Grucci and John T'Lustachowski
Information Editor: Tatiana Shohov
Book Production: Donna Dennis, Patrick Davin, Christine Mathosian, Tammy Sauter
and Diane Sharp
Circulation: Maryanne Schmidt
Marketing/Sales: Cathy DeGregory

Library of Congress Cataloging-in-Publication Data
available upon request

ISBN 1-56072-397-1

CONTENTS

CHAPTER 1

A NEW APPROACH TO DREAM INTERPRETATION

Dreams have been a mystery since the dawn of time.

You've undoubtedly sensed there are important messages for you in your dreams. Yet you haven't known a reliable way to identify what those messages are.

Despite the best efforts of countless dream interpreters down through history, the public remains ignorant of what dreams mean or how to interpret them.

That's all coming to an end.

In this book you'll learn a new dream analysis system which can pinpoint meanings in even your most complex dreams, and which can make many of your dreams utterly easy to interpret. Furthermore, you won't need a therapist to help you apply it to your dreams. **You'll be able to interpret your dreams on your own!**

The basic concept that system revolves around is this: dreams begin by showing what the dreamer loves, continue in the early-middle plot with what is desired, proceed in the late-middle section with what is undesirable, and end by revealing what is hated.

Those are inner emotions being depicted rather than conscious ones, so many of those dream feelings will prove surprising when one analyzes them afterwards. And as we shall see in this book, some of them will be shocking.

Nevertheless, you'll find that being able to understand your dreams is a lifeline to good judgment and emotional stability. That's because the messages in your dreams typically reflect a person inside you with adaptive qualities such as intelligence, benevolence, and resourcefulness.

In fact, being able to understand your dreams can mean the difference between adapting well to life or instead committing horrendous blunders which could lead to all sorts of misfortune.

For example, suppose you've been planning something major such as a marriage or a career change. Your inner self will give you important feedback about it in one or more of your dreams. **If you dream about that planned life change in a dream's beginning or early-middle section, the inner message is one of approval; if you instead dream about it in a late-middle section or in the dream's ending, the inner message being communicated is disapproval.**

In that way, your dreams give you guidance about all the important trends in your life.

There's more to learn about dream interpretation, of course, and the several hundred dream examples in the following chapters provide a basic illustration of underlying mechanisms you will find in your own dreams.

Reader, are you receptive to innovation?

The theory that dreams follow a love-desire-nondesire-hatred pattern is totally different from all past approaches to dream interpretation. Why that should be so is a considerable surprise, since many dreams quite obviously display that emotional sequence. (Others seemingly don't, and a number of those are analyzed in Chapter Three.) In any case, what you'll read about in this book has met with opposition from people in the dream interpretation "establishment."

But resistance to new concepts dwindles and then disappears when those concepts turn out to be valid.

After you've read the next three chapters, you'll be able to understand many of your dreams. The middle chapters in the book explain dream complications. The final chapters are designed to deepen your understanding of dream interpretation.

I'd wish you good luck in relation to understanding your dreams, but after you've read the explanations and examples in this book you won't need that luck. You'll be able to rely on rational analysis instead.

Remember that it's up to you to draw your own independent conclusions about what you learn in the following chapters.

CHAPTER 2

DREAM PATTERN INTERPRETATION

Accurate dream interpretation can be amazingly simple. The basic procedure is always the same. Take a complete dream and analyze its four separate parts, using the "blueprint" that the dreamer's inner self loves what is shown in the dream's beginning, desires what is in the early-middle location, finds undesirable the contents of the late-middle plot, and hates what appears in the ending.

Carrying out that process provides the complete meaning of many dreams. It helps us understand the following four dreams, for example.

1. A man dreamed this:

I went horseback riding. The horse took me through beautiful countryside. When it was time to go back I chose a different way, became lost, and came to some barbed wire that blocked the path. The horse became restless and tried to throw me.

The man goes horseback riding at the beginning of his dream, and therefore he loves doing that. Riding through beautiful countryside appears in the early-middle part of the dream, so he desires that scenery. The late-middle plot shows him becoming lost and then finding the way blocked by barbed wire. Those situations are identified by their location within his dream as being undesirable to him. The dream ending reveals he would hate it if a horse tried to throw him.

Those are normal, unsurprising emotions, and might seem disappointing for that reason. Shouldn't all dreams reflect the soul's mysteries? An answer is that the dreamer said he hadn't been horseback riding for too long, and dreaming about it was enjoyable.

2. A woman dreamed the following:

I am buying jewels in a jewelry store. I choose a big pendant necklace with emeralds, flashing and beautiful. When I try it on, it hangs down too far, so I give it to my sister. She gives it back. She has nothing green to wear with it. She wants blue.

The dream messages are apparent at first glance. The woman loves buying jewelry. She desires buying an emerald necklace. It would be undesirable if the necklace didn't fit her and she ended up giving it to her sister. She would hate it if her sister rejected her gift because of a petulant demand about the necklace's color.

3. A female guitarist dreamed this:

I was in the street watching people play the guitar and sing. These two guys started playing. They sounded real good. They had a magic sound. Beautiful. The crowd stood up and cheered. It made me think that some people have it and some don't. I wasn't sure that I had it. As I was walking home, I was thinking I could find out if the crowd liked me by performing in front of them, but I was afraid. Afraid of rejection.

Her inner emotions about performers and performing are clear. She would love watching people play the guitar and sing. It would be desirable to watch men perform who sang and played beautifully. She also would desire that the audience cheer the men, so she seems inclined to have benevolent wishes toward people who satisfy her desires. It would be undesirable to her inner self if she consciously were to believe that she lacked sufficient musical talent. And she inwardly would hate being unwilling to perform in front of others because of a conscious fear of rejection.

4. A woman who taught elementary students dreamed the following:

I had a picnic for the kids in my class and most of them showed up. Ralph, my favorite student, brought a watermelon. While they were playing, one of the girls scratched her knee on the hedge and I took her in to the bathroom to put merthiolate on the scratch. When we got back outside I saw that the children were throwing watermelon slices at each other. I had to go around and take the remaining watermelon away from them. Later, after we'd cooked dinner and eaten it, the mothers came for their children and the picnic came to an end.

These are nice emotions for a teacher to have. She would love being on a picnic with her schoolchildren. She also would love it if her favorite student brought a watermelon to that picnic. (Probably she would love not only the watermelon but also the affection she would feel toward him as a consequence. She would love feeling love, in other words.) She desires being helpful to the children, such as by putting merthiolate on a child's scratched knee. It would be undesirable if the children misbehaved and thereby compelled her to punish them. She would hate it when the picnic came to an end.

Will other dreams be as easy to interpret as these four have been? Not always. There are potential misunderstandings even when the inner self has been as straightforward as possible in presenting dream messages.

For example, one has to divide the dream into its four separate parts before proceeding with the interpretation, and of course it's possible to make mistakes while doing so. The middle of a long dream might contain a scene about buying lottery tickets, for example, and one might decide doing so is desirable when it instead is undesirable. Fortunately, when you're analyzing your own dreams such mistakes needn't happen. Your logic and intuition can tell you the emotional significance of a dream event which seems to be in an ambiguous location, and even in the longest dreams the beginning of each new dream section can be obvious to you.

Trying to separate other people's dreams into the four parts often involves much uncertainty, however, and it may prove difficult (or impossible) to determine the emotional significance of particular dream material until one has questioned the dreamer.

These next two examples illustrate that questioning process.

A woman told me this dream:

I am at a diet club meeting. So many women are there it's held in a gym. Everybody has to line up along a numbered line like I used to do in my tenth grade gym class. My number is 101. The leader is late, and we have to wait a long time.

Virtually all of this dream was immediately obvious to me. The dreamer loves her diet club meetings. She desires both that a lot of women attend and that the meetings be held in a gym. If everyone had to line up along a numbered line it would be undesirable if her number was 101, which presumably would place her in a position at the rear of the group. She would hate it if the group's leader was late and they had to wait a long time for that person to show up.

I wasn't sure how to classify the part about lining up along a numbered line. Based on its location in the dream it could be either desirable or undesirable to her, and her past experiences could cause her to feel either emotion about it. So I asked her, "Did you like to line up along numbered lines when you were in your tenth grade physical education class?"

"Oh, yes," she said. "It was fun to trade numbers so I could be with my friends."

I concluded that lining up along a numbered line had appeared in the desire section of her dream, since she remembered it as being enjoyable.

A boy told me this dream:

My father, older brother, and I were in a canoe on a stream inside a cave. There were artificial lights in the ceiling. A monster was chasing us. My father was throwing up in the water. My paddle slipped out of my hands and it drifted away out of reach.

Presumably, the boy had been in a canoe inside a cave in the past, and had loved it. In that setting, he would desire artificial lighting in the ceiling, since the light in the cave otherwise would be dim. It would be undesirable if his father were sick, and he would hate losing his paddle.

Would it be desirable or undesirable for a monster to chase the three of them? My immediate reaction was that being chased by a monster would be undesirable. Then it occurred to me that if one is in the company of one's father and older brother, being chased by a monster might be exciting, and therefore desirable, rather than ominous.

I asked the boy, "How do you think you'd feel about being chased by a monster if you were with your father and brother?"

"That would give me a chance to show them I could act like Tarzan," he replied, and I decided the dream chase had appeared in his desire section.

There seems more to consider in relation to that dream. Part of the Freudian legacy is a pervasive awareness that dreams can contain symbols, and several people I discussed that dream with assumed that the monster was symbolic. Indeed, were there anxiety-producing elements in the boy's life which caused him to dream of that pursuer? And if so, should the boy, under the guidance of a therapist, try to come to terms with his anxiety?

Such questions can be good ones, of course. Here, though, there's nothing to suggest any grim realities contributed to the dream, since the messages in it seem normal and the boy hadn't reported it as being a nightmare. In general, dream monsters can simply be monsters and nothing more, especially when they have a desirable aspect to them.

This next example involving classification of dream content similarly touches upon a question of symbolism. A girl dreamed:

I was out in the country at a baby-sitter's house. I had to go to the bathroom and went to the outdoor privy. When I opened the door of the privy, I saw a bunch of snakes on the dirt floor. They chased me to the house. I couldn't get the door of the house open and the snakes were about to touch me.

The snakes in that dream may seem symbolic, especially to those versed in the concepts of sexual repression and censorship. Did those snakes have an underlying sexual significance, and reflect the girl's potential fear of being chased by men? Perhaps, but it would be premature to make that assumption based on the "evidence" of just this dream. If the girl had that fear, other dreams of hers also would reflect it.

We see that the girl loved being at the baby-sitter's house. It was desirable to her to use the outdoor bathroom there, probably because of its novelty to her. It would be undesirable to find snakes in that bathroom, and she would hate it if she couldn't open the door to the house and the snakes were about to get her.

It's unclear if being chased by snakes appeared in her dream's nondesire section or instead in the hatred section. Yet a precise answer to this uncertainty might not be important, since in either instance the message would be that she had a negative feeling about being chased by snakes. Similarly, an exact classification might not be necessary regarding material which is midway in the first half of a dream, and therefore is something the dreamer either loves or desires. But material in the very center of a dream must be classified accurately, of course, since the distinction will be whether something is desirable or instead is undesirable.

As the next two examples show, sometimes it's necessary to read between the lines in analyzing dream messages, as otherwise one would miss some of the message.

A woman dreamed this in the last half of a dream:

My husband's boss told my husband that he was cutting his wages to $1.00 an hour, and if he didn't like it he was fired. So we began packing our suitcases. We were having quite a time getting the shoes in.

The dreamer was not truly concerned that her husband would have to quit his job and they would have to relocate elsewhere. This is shown by the relatively trivial nature of the hatred material. Being unable to fit shoes into a suitcase is not a frustration the inner self will focus on if it sees worse possibilities ahead.

A female real estate broker dreamed the following:

I was called to appraise a house. It turned out to have western-style architecture. The floor was littered with Cheerios and the owner was mean and uncooperative.

It seems unlikely that a house she appraised would actually have Cheerios on the floor, so why had she dreamed that improbable plot? "What associations do you have to Cheerios on the floor?" I asked her.

"My two-year-old daughter often spills them on the floor while she's eating her breakfast," she answered. Those spilled Cheerios were undesirable to her, and her dream was combining that message with the more obvious one that it would be undesirable for a house she appraised to be littered. As well, that nondesire section, when viewed against the rest of the dream, seems to be revealing a concern the woman has over how to integrate her work and her home life.

Is the rest of that dream clear to you? The dreamer loves being called to appraise houses, she likes houses with western-style architecture, and she would hate it if the owner of a house turned out to be a grouch.

A potential pitfall occurs when dreams reflect mixed feelings toward someone, since the interpreter might become confused about those feelings. That happened to me with this next example. A woman wrote to me about a series of recurring dreams she had, beginning when she was a teenager and continuing for the next thirty years:

The setting is the Mardi Gras in New Orleans. I am young, beautiful, and dressed as a Southern belle. There are colorful floats, noise, and music; the streets are crowded with the parade. Sometimes I'm weaving my way through the crowd on foot, and sometimes I'm in a float, smiling and waving. Or I might be in a buggy drawn by horses. I always meet this same handsome man with black hair and eyes. He also is in a costume of some sort. Sometimes we are together as lovers. Sometimes I spend much of the dream searching for him. Then, after we find each other, we either part or one of us gets lost from the other. Sometimes I'm in a cemetery, searching for names on the monuments. At times this man appears, only to embrace me and leave again. I

wake up lonely and wondering who that man is. Will we ever meet again?

The dreamer would love participating in the festivities of the Mardi Gras, especially as a young, beautiful belle. The handsome man is an object of desire to her. Once they were together, becoming separated from him would be undesirable.

Those emotions were easy to interpret, but her account of the ending of some of the recurring dreams left me wondering. Did the handsome stranger's appearance in the hatred section of some of her dreams mean that in addition to desiring him she also hated him? Or was his appearance in those dream endings only a necessary prelude to his subsequent disappearance, and was the hatred message simply that she would hate his leaving? What, furthermore, was the significance of his appearing in a cemetery?

I wrote to the woman explaining my interpretations of the first three parts of her recurring dreams, and admitted that I was unsure how to interpret the endings. "What associations do you have to that man?" I asked her in my letter.

She wrote back, "I've often wondered if he represented my father, who also had black hair and eyes. He left when I was five, and I never saw or heard from him again. I grew up wondering about him, and longing to see him again."

Now the meaning of her dream endings became clearer to me. That handsome man sometimes was a symbol for her father. She had felt some hatred toward him for leaving, and his symbolic presence in the hatred sections reflected that hatred. Yet the search for names in the cemetery indicated her hatred of finding out he was dead, implying she still wanted to meet him. Her unresolved feelings about her father, furthermore, apparently caused her to wish at times for a lover who resembled him. Overall, her feelings were complicated ones, and the dreams were reflecting her mixture of desire and hatred for that composite figure.

Opposing feelings won't necessarily be complicated ones, however. For example, a woman dreamed this in her desire section:

The husband of my best friend began to make a pass at me. At first I enjoyed it but then out of loyalty to my friend I pushed him away.

Since both these events occurred in her dream's desire section, the related conclusion is that she desired both the pass from her friend's husband and the moral strength to resist him.

Some dreams can mislead the interpreter because an initial setting continues to be depicted in the plot even though the dream pattern messages are no longer about that setting. For instance, a female college student dreamed this:

My dormitory room is an aquarium with water everywhere. Fish are swimming about in the room. I'm lying on the bed and my hair is floating straight up. Bubbles are coming out of my mouth.

The woman said she had an aquarium in her dormitory room and enjoyed watching the fish swim around in it. With that information, it becomes clear the first half of her dream is showing an enjoyable fantasy about her entire room being an aquarium. What does the second half reveal, however? If the dreamer were underwater, it would be natural both for her hair to float up and for bubbles to come out of her mouth. Why then did the first of these occurrences appear in the nondesire part of her dream and the second show up in her dream's hatred section?

Perhaps the last half of her dream was representing "abovewater" messages. That realization helped me ask the right questions.

"Does your hair ever 'float up' when you are in your dormitory room?"

She nodded. "Sometimes I take naps in my room during the day, and when I do, my hair usually gets mussed up."

That was the nondesire problem identified. "And do you ever have difficulty breathing?"

"I have asthma attacks sometimes."

That solved the mystery of what she hated. The bubbles symbolized the labored breathing she experienced during her asthma attacks. She hated those breathing problems.

The question remains of why her dream continued to portray her as being underwater, even though her nondesire and hatred messages didn't have anything to do with that situation at all. Probably her inner self had chosen to continue that enjoyable scene in order to be kind to her.

A similar instance follows in which a dream extended a loved setting into the desire section and beyond, although at the risk of making those subsequent messages less clear. A 13-year-old boy dreamed this:

I was throwing rocks into a puddle of water. Then I saw the image of a beautiful woman in the water. But as I looked, she became ugly and then started to reach toward me. I ran away.

That image of a beautiful woman in the water was a clever way of showing what the dreamer desired without abandoning the background scene he loved.

There is another potential complication regarding the interpretation of this dream. It would seem natural to run away from the menace the ugly woman poses, yet dreams theoretically end with hatred. Should the interpreter overlook that theory and assume the ending was revealing the boy's likely response to the undesirable situation?

"How do you feel about running away?" I asked the boy.

"I hate it," he quickly replied. Running away was incompatible with his views regarding manliness.

Here is another example of a dream which readily could be misinterpreted. A woman reported that as a child she had dreamed this in the last half of a dream:

I was falling and falling. I was terrified. And I wanted to scream, but was unable to do so.

It might appear that the urge to scream was related to falling. The dreamer had a different explanation, though: "As a child," she said, "I was not permitted to express my feelings. It wasn't until I was 16 that I began speaking out." Thus the wish to scream was a consequence of being forced to suppress her emotions.

What can be learned from these three examples? Sometimes either a dream setting or one's perceptions of it can be influenced by the preceding dream plot in a potentially confusing or misleading way. Therefore, it is important to remember that each new dream section presents a message that might be entirely unrelated to the previous plot, no matter how closely it seems to fit in with it.

The concepts you learn in this book about dream interpretation can be applied both to your own dreams and to those of others. When you analyze your own dreams, the personal context of what you've dreamed is accessible to you, and so the interpretations can illuminate your inner feelings and provide rich implications. We've already seen some of the practical difficulties in trying to interpret the dreams of others, though. The inevitable obstacle lies in obtaining sufficient information to make complete interpretations. Without that information, what remains might be just a minimal analysis.

The remaining two examples in this chapter illustrate a success and a failure, respectively, in dream interpretation. In the first instance, the dreamer was available for me to question. That wasn't so when I tried to analyze the second dream, though.

A woman reported having had the following dream during her childhood:

I was being held prisoner in a yellow castle. The other prisoners--not visible in the dream but I somehow knew about them--were periodically being forced to commit suicide. I knew I'd be next if I didn't escape. So I climbed out of a window. There was a thick forest outside the castle, and I ended up lost in it.

"I don't see a sequence of love, desire, nondesire, and hatred in that," she said after she had told me the dream.

"When you were a child," I asked her, "did you sometimes feel like a prisoner at home?"

She nodded. "My parents were strict authoritarians and I often felt like a prisoner."

"So in comparison with being a prisoner at home, you evidently would have loved being held prisoner in a yellow castle. Did you like the color yellow?"

She chuckled. "The yellow stones in the castle in my dream were pretty."

"Did you have any brothers or sisters?"

"I had four brothers."

"Did you have any trouble getting along with them?"

"Yes. They were all older than I was and were always trying to tell me what to do."

"They apparently were symbolized by those other prisoners in the dream. Because your brothers tried to order you around, it was desirable to you that they experience an unhappy fate--at least in the dream. As for escaping from the castle, this occurred in the nondesire section of your dream, and presumably presented the real-life message that it would have been undesirable for you to run away from home, although you might have thought about doing so at times. The dream ends with you lost in a forest. I'm not sure if it is just being lost that you would have hated, or whether you would have hated wandering about in a forest. Did you have any unpleasant experiences with forests as a child?"

"I went to girl scout camp and there were some peacocks in the woods that scared me. I asked to sleep in a tent in the middle of the camp, with all the other tents between me and the woods, so that the peacocks wouldn't get me." She laughed. "Maybe your dream pattern theory makes sense after all."

Here are the early-middle and late-middle sections of a teenage girl's dream:

I was driving the family car, and a friend was with me. The car in front of us suddenly swerved to the right and stopped. A man jumped out and ran to the middle of the road. We realized it was a police car, and the man was a policeman. Because of the ice I had been driving slowly, and the policeman managed to run to the door on my side and try to open it. I attempted to lock the door but couldn't. The policeman opened the door and ran alongside the car until I finally stopped. He pointed a gun at me and tried to get me out of the car. I

refused and he shot me in the left leg. "Now you can't drive," he said. "Yes, I can," I answered. "You shot me in the wrong leg."

The dream pattern messages are: (1) the girl desired that a policeman try to stop her from driving; and (2) it would have been undesirable for the policeman's efforts to fail. The analysis shouldn't end there, though. Why did she have those emotions? Was her inner self concerned about some aspect of her driving? Did she instead feel an inner reluctance to arrive at the destination? Where did she usually go with that friend, and what usually happened after she got there? Finding answers to such questions is important when a dream depicts inner concern. What is that concern about, and how can it be resolved?

I don't have those answers. The girl had sent me that dream by mail, and she didn't reply when I wrote back, providing the above interpretations and asking for clarifications. (I don't blame her, of course. She was a teenager and I was an inquisitive adult, seemingly aligned with the forces that might seek to curtail her driving privileges.)

Regarding that dream, you may have noticed that at a surface level the early-middle event of being stopped by a policeman doesn't seem desirable, nor does the late-middle plot of continuing to drive seem undesirable. Now you may be wondering whether desire and nondesire messages were indeed being presented. In general, do all dreams follow the love-desire-nondesire-hatred pattern, or, as this example might seem to indicate, do some dreams deviate from it?

The next chapter will answer this important question.

CHAPTER 3

DO ALL DREAMS FOLLOW THE SAME PATTERN?

Do all dreams follow the love-desire-nondesire-hatred pattern? Not always, since noises can disrupt the dream plot, and so can other external stimuli. That dream continues, but not in the way the inner mind had planned. The intended messages are lost, and it's a waste of time to try to interpret the resulting plot, which primarily reflects the distracting element in the outer world.

At least, though, dreams always try to include those four consecutive emotions. I concluded this right from the start. My own dreams never voluntarily switched from that emotional pattern, and why would other people's dreams be any different? Admittedly, when I first began talking with other people about their dreams I had a few anxious moments.

For example, a woman told me a dream that began with her working as a waitress. Many women who work at that occupation don't love it. "How do you feel about being a waitress?" I asked her, wondering if she would respond in a lukewarm or negative way.

"Oh, I love it," she answered.

A woman dreamed in the early-middle plot that she met the wife of a man she was having an affair with. I couldn't imagine why she would dream about that meeting in what, theoretically, was the desire section. "What do you feel toward that woman?" I asked her.

"I like her," she answered. That was why she desired meeting her.

A woman told me a dream about driving on mountain roads, and ended her account this way:

And then a rock came down from the mountain and hit my windshield and cracked it, but didn't break it.

If that was the end of her dream, it was the hatred section, yet why would she hate the rock cracking her car's windshield but not breaking it? Wouldn't she instead hate her windshield being broken? Her dream seemed to have, if not a happy ending, at least one that didn't contain a situation she hated. I wondered if the pillars of my universe were beginning to crumble.

It turned out the dreamer had an explanation: "Something like that did happen," she said, "and I drove with a cracked windshield for two weeks. Finally I couldn't stand it any longer and had the entire windshield replaced. It would have been better if the rock had broken my windshield at the start, rather than just cracking it. That way I wouldn't have had the aggravation of driving with a cracked windshield for two weeks."

So her dream ending was showing something she hated after all.

Another woman told me this dream:

I drove up to a small house with evergreen bushes in front of the porch. I noticed parts of the bushes were bright yellow, orange, and maple red. I looked more closely and found some orange-reddish material in a cloth bag. I saw more material, colored beige-pink with white polka dots, and put that in the bag, too. I took the bag to the car and saw on the back seat a folder with documents that needed sorting out.

While I was wondering whether her dream actually followed my pattern (and if so, what it meant), she told me her associations to it. She said she loved the colors of autumn, such as the ones displayed at the beginning of the dream. She had liked the orange-reddish material, but hadn't cared as much for the beige-pink material. The end of the dream reminded her of several boxes of papers that she had to sort out, although she wasn't looking forward to doing so.

It hadn't occurred to me that orange-red material could be desirable and beige-pink material could instead be undesirable. Also, her associations indicated why the beginning and ending of her dream were feelings of love and hatred.

Sometimes the people who told me their dreams subsequently would disagree with my interpretations. Was that proof that their dreams didn't follow my pattern? I will provide several examples and let you judge the validity of their objections.

A man told me this dream:

The Rolling Stones were in my living room. The stereo was playing a Gershwin melody. The music was really nice but then it came to an end. The Rolling Stones seemed to be in a meditative mood.

I interpreted the dream to him. "You'd love for the Rolling Stones to be in your living room, but you'd desire that the stereo play a Gershwin record. Therefore, you want the Rolling Stones to be in your living room for some other reason than to hear their music. The ending of the dream-- the hatred section--provides a clue what that other reason would be. You'd hate for them to be in a meditative mood, and this suggests that you'd prefer watching them display their stage boisterousness and charisma."

The man thought for a few seconds. "I wouldn't hate for the Rolling Stones to be meditative."

"But if they were in your living room, wouldn't you want them to have the same personalities as they do on stage?"

"I suppose so. But I wouldn't hate it if they were meditative," he repeated.

That was his final answer. I couldn't convince him that he might feel differently inside.

A man with spiritual interests was telling me about a dream of his. "It ended with me bowing down to the guru and kissing his feet," he said.

"You'd hate doing that."

"I would not!" He seemed shocked. "I would love doing it as an expression of my gratitude to him for showing me the correct way."

I wasn't in a deprogramming mood. "Okay," I said.

A teen-age girl told me about a dream of hers.

I walked barefoot to the porch to get something for my mother. I saw a huge brown spider and jumped on a chair and screamed for help. The spider jumped on my back, and people tried to get it off but it remained on my back.

"You like to go barefoot, don't you?" I asked the girl.

"Yes," she said, smiling.

"And you also like to fetch things for your mother."

"No, I don't," she quickly said. We were on a bus and several of her friends were sitting nearby, listening.

"You don't? But the beginning of your dream--"

"No," she said firmly. Her friends laughed.

She might have responded differently to my interpretation if we had been alone, but how many teenagers can publicly admit that they love to help their mother?

It may seem strange, incidentally, that the desire plot showed her seeing a spider. She screamed for help after she saw it, though. The related message is that she desires the attention such a scream would bring.

A woman dreamed the following, which included a stressful conflict in the love section:

I was in the garage, and saw a rat go across the floor. It was slow, and so I was able to pick it up at the back of its neck. I held it and yelled for my husband to come and kill it. He took a long time coming, and I almost lost it a time or two. It tried to bite and scratch me, and I was afraid it might have broken the skin. I was afraid it might be carrying some disease. Finally, my husband arrived, but he couldn't find anything to kill it with. At last he found a hatchet. But he didn't do anything about the rat. Instead he found a picture and put it up on the wall in the garage. Then he began looking for more pictures to put on the kitchen cabinet doors. It was hard to keep a grip on the rat. Then my husband sat down and went to sleep. He couldn't seem to wake up long enough to know what he was doing. There was a plate on the table, and I began banging it, trying to get his attention. Finally, I threw the plate on the floor and it broke in two pieces. That still didn't

wake him enough to kill the rat. But then he awakened and either began looking for things, nails or pictures or the hammer, or was just standing around, not doing anything. My feelings were of great frustration toward him. He seemed incapable of understanding my need or the situation.

The beginning of this dream shows the dreamer catching a rat with her bare hands and waiting a long time for her husband to come and kill it, and as she waits the rat squirms in her hands and almost manages to bite or scratch her. Why would she love this grim situation?

The woman's husband is depicted unfavorably throughout the dream, and the logical conclusion is that she feels latent hostility toward him. Such hostility seeks the chance to surface, and so she would love having a good excuse to become angry with them. She'd have that excuse if he took a long time to respond to an emergency, and that is the reason for the prolonged struggle with the rat in her dream's beginning.

All in all, that dream is an instructive one. The desire and nondesire sections show how dreams can weave secondary messages in with a predominant one. The primary theme, of course, is that she has negative feelings for her husband. The secondary message in the desire section is that she likes for him to put up pictures, and the secondary message in the late-middle plot is that it's undesirable to break plates.

The hatred section reveals she would hate to feel frustrated about her husband, yet the beginning of her dream shows she would love having a good reason to resent him. There isn't much difference between those two feelings, and it becomes apparent that when an emotion is warped, as the love is in this instance, it can cause related emotions to become conflicting or contradictory.

We see a similar example in the dream that follows of dream material showing up in a seemingly inappropriate location. This time, though, the reason isn't abnormal emotions but instead a wish to change dissatisfying reality. A man dreamed in the late-middle part of a dream:

Papa got into the storm cellar and was going to close the door. I said, "Wait a minute," and took another look outside and saw a great wall of water coming at us. I got in with Papa and closed the door and put

my arm around him and said, "I love you, Papa," and he said, "I love you, too."

This scenario carries a nondesire message because of its location. What is undesirable, though, about the dreamer and his father saying they loved each other? It turned out that his father had died several years before, and the dreamer hadn't told him he loved him before that death occurred. The dream was implying the man's regret about what he had failed to do in real life. At the same time, it was helping him cope with his regret by giving him that constructive fantasy.

That dream was providing excellent "therapy," of course, and we shall see numerous other examples in this book of dreams which help the dreamer cope with a difficult or dismal reality.

If one didn't look beneath the surface, this next dream might seem to have a happy ending. A woman dreamed:

I am in an empty old hotel. I have inherited it from someone famous--maybe Buffalo Bill. I'm standing in the bare room, oak floors, large windows, sunshine, warm breezes. I am in a beautiful, white, floor-length summer gown. I am in the body of an old school friend whom I thought was attractive. Enter a man named Henry--another school chum, but someone I was less fond of, except in the dream he's tall, sensual, appealing. He takes me in his arms and tells me that Black Bart has discovered he can lay claim to the hotel if I am not married. I am upset at the idea of losing the hotel. So Henry asks me to marry him, and we go to the justice of the peace and all ends well.

The dream ending shows the woman marrying, for financial reasons, a man whom she hasn't liked in the past, and it seems to predict they would live happily ever after. That plot occurs in the hatred section, though, and the true message is that she would hate such a forced marriage. The indirect guidance is that she should marry for love rather than money.

Note that the dream presents the character of Henry in the nondesire and hatred sections, yet also must include him in the desire section for the sake of the plot's continuity. In order for Henry to appear in her desire section, however, he has to change, and so he becomes physically desirable. Creative? Yes, but dictated by necessity. As this illustrates, the transformations which people undergo in dreams are not random or whimsical, but instead occur for essential reasons.

This next example also seems at first glance to have a happy ending. An overweight woman who had been having problems staying on a diet dreamed this in the last half of a dream:

I recited: "I like peanut butter and jelly. I like peanut butter and jam. I like peanut butter and mustard. But I like myself just as I am." And then I laughed heartily.

Hearty laughter in the hatred section? What is going on? And what is the related meaning of the seemingly nonsensical words the dreamer speaks?

New theory follows to help with this analysis.

WHEN A DREAM CHARACTER BECOMES EMOTIONAL

There are two separate types of feelings a dream character can display. One type, unsurprisingly, is genuine. The other is opposite to emotional reality. **A figure showing this latter feeling will smile or laugh to reveal pain and cry to indicate happiness.** Fortunately, it's not difficult to distinguish between the two varieties. A reliable general rule (derived from the close study of many dreams) is that any character in a dream who is emotional while speaking will be conveying a genuine feeling, and any emotional character who either doesn't speak at all or doesn't speak while displaying the emotion will be conveying an opposite-to-reality feeling.

Returning to our example, we see that the woman's image spoke and then laughed, but the laughter didn't overlap with the speech. Therefore her amusement in the dream wasn't genuine, and implied that reality contained considerable amounts of pain for her. If the pain were less, she might have been shown as smiling rather than laughing.

What was her pain about? Her words in the nondesire section held a clue. They depicted a frivolous complacency about her eating habits. It was undesirable for her to like herself as she was--someone who ate the wrong foods and too much of them--and instead she should want to change.

The dream laughter's location in her hatred section indicates she hated the pain reality held for her. That pain was caused by her conscious choices regarding eating, so a related assumption is that she was on the verge of hating herself. Overall, the merriment in her dream, opposite to her reality, had ominous implications.

Admittedly, the concept of opposite-to-reality feelings in the dream plot is a difficult one to grasp immediately. Three more examples of it follow now, and a number of additional examples will be presented in Chapter Five.

A man who was unemployed by choice dreamed in the ending of a dream that he felt love about his lifestyle. No words accompanied that love, so it wasn't genuine to him. What was its purpose in his hatred section? The dream was indicating that being out of work hadn't caused the man to feel love, and as a consequence he would hate loving the jobless situation which was proving unrewarding to him. One assumes he initially had loved the prospect of not working, but now was changing.

A woman who had been mourning the poor health of a friend bedridden by a stroke and paralysis dreamed this in the love section of a dream:

I was called to a funeral home to be told Roberta had died. My reaction to that was hatred of her death.

Strange as it might seem, the dreamer would love that death if she could also hate it. Roberta hadn't died yet, though, so the dreamer wasn't feeling that hatred in real life.

The desire section of that same dream helped clarify her complicated feelings about wishing for her friend's death. She dreamed in the early-middle plot that the funeral director said to her, "Oh, it's not your Roberta." Those words would be comforting to hear, and were reflecting an inner perspective that the ailing person whose death would be a mercy was someone entirely different from the healthy friend Roberta had been.

A youth in a detention home dreamed this in the nondesire section:

I began walking toward the fence. I was going to try to escape. Then I heard music. It wasn't being played over a loudspeaker but instead somehow was playing just for me. It was peaceful yet inspiring music, and I sensed it was "music to make my escape by."

How do you suppose the youth's inner self felt about the prospect of escaping from the detention home? Hint: the emotionally-tinged music was conveying an opposite-to-reality feeling.

The dream's message was that it would have been undesirable to try to escape. The peaceful, inspiring music was implying that if the youth did make that attempt he inwardly would feel tense rather than peaceful and depressed rather than inspired.

From now on, when you examine your dreams you will be able to spot the emotional pattern in them, even if opposite-to-reality feelings are present. Recognizing that pattern is an enormous step, since it can lead you to an immediate understanding of the related messages. Those messages will be from your inner self, and without dream pattern analysis they might never reach your conscious awareness.

Are those inner messages worth paying attention to? The answer, of course, is yes. In fact, sometimes it is hard to understand how people can survive without them.

CHAPTER 4

HOW DREAMS HELP US ADAPT

Cats, dogs, elephants, and chimpanzees dream. But is it likely that even the most intelligent of these animals would be able to think analytically about their dreams? Probably not, and there logically should be another reason that dreams occur besides the chance afterwards that the dreamer could analyze the messages. Mother Nature wouldn't waste the ability to dream.

In fact, dreams influence the dreamer at a level of emotion and spontaneous imagination, and they are never wasted. Here is how that process works. What you dream about won't necessarily happen, but if it does, you'll involuntarily feel an accompanying emotion of love, desire, nondesire, or hatred, depending on where in the dream that situation appeared. Furthermore, imagining even at a level below conscious thought that a dreamed-about situation is coming true will evoke some of that same feeling. Love and desire are pleasant to feel, of course, and nondesire and hatred are painful. Dreaming influences you, therefore, to bring about those situations which appear in the first half of your dreams and to avoid those appearing in the last half.

It is also part of nature's plan that dreams don't push the dreamer in the wrong direction. As we shall see in this chapter, they contain constructive adaptations which reflect a deep understanding of the dreamer's true realities.

LOVING IN FANTASY AND REALITY

A woman dreamed this in the beginning of a dream:

There are some refugee children in a run-down, dirty house. I befriend seven or eight of them and take them to my big house. I return to the other house, and there are some more children there. They want to sneak into my group.

The woman is being influenced to love helping children. She undoubtedly is inclined to feel motherly toward them, as otherwise this love would be wrong for her. Note that the dream is also causing her to love being popular with children. Dream sections such as this one with twists and turns in the plot inevitably have more than one subsequent influence upon the dreamer.

This was the beginning of a man's dream:

I was applying for a summer job at a refinery, and had to stop at a security gate such as all refineries have. I passed some pleasantries with the guard before going on to the interview.

The dreamer had an employment interview at a refinery scheduled for the following day, and the dream beginning was helping him love that interview and as well any sociability he could engage in before it began. It is clear the man's inner self approved of the potential job, since it depicted the interview as something to love. Nor is it surprising that the love section showed him being friendly with the guard, since people innately love such positive social interactions. Yet there may have been a practical reason for including that friendliness in the plot. Did he foresee at an inner level that he would be in a good mood after being pleasant to the guard, and consequently would be more likely to make a favorable impression during the interview? Dreams sometimes do contain that sort of farsighted logic.

SENSIBLE DESIRES

A ten-year-old girl dreamed in her dream's desire section that she was holding a baby in her arms. By giving her that desire, her inner self was preparing her to adapt to a motherly role, presumably as a baby-sitter and ultimately with her own children.

A woman dreamed in the desire section that she was shaking her son, but not losing control of her emotions. The woman occasionally did shake her son after he misbehaved, and there was a danger that at such times she might, in an excess of temper, shake him too violently. To prevent that abusive situation from occurring, her inner self was causing her to desire that she remain in control of her temper.

Here is a more pleasant desire plot, and the adaptation it reflects is what some psychologists would call a "peak experience." After dreaming at the beginning of a dream of being at a swimming pool with his wife and another couple, a man dreamed in the desire section:

The other three were sunbathing and I was clowning around while jumping off the high diving board. I was doing can openers and cannonballs, trying to soak them. Finally a guard told me to knock it off, so on my next dive I did a perfect swan dive.

The desire material displayed the man's playful urge to soak his wife and friends. That playfulness could become excessive, however, so the plot added a desire to be responsive to authority when told to stop those antics. Also, the man's inner self may have seen that if he performed only the graceless dives his self image would suffer: the desire section wisely included the wish to dive gracefully after finishing the bellyfloppers.

THE DEPICTION OF SEXUAL DESIRE

Desire sections can be about sex, of course, and when they are they identify sexual turn-ons for the dreamer. That sexual desire won't necessarily be based on physical attractiveness. Personality factors also contribute to physical desire.

The next example illustrates this influence of personality on desire. A man worked with a woman who was friendly and cooperative. She had small breasts, and the man had women friends whose breasts were larger. Yet one night he dreamed in his desire section that he was with this woman he worked with, and she was topless. He could see her naked breasts, and they were realistically shown in his dream as being small.

What was the motive involved in causing him to desire her breasts? Evidently, his inner self thought this woman would be an excellent girlfriend for him because of her positive personal qualities, and therefore produced the desire which would help him be sexually attracted to her.

Dreams can affect physiological functioning as well as emotions and behavior. When a sexual situation dreamed about in the desire section occurs in real life, adult dreamers who have no distracting concerns will feel immediate or increased sexual desire, and also will experience the physiological correlates of sexual arousal. So what do you suppose would probably happen if the man who dreamed that last example were alone with that woman he'd dreamed about, and she smiled at him and removed her blouse? The likely initial event, which wouldn't involve any conscious choice on his part, would be that he'd have an erection. His body would be responding to the dream message that her breasts were desirable.

Sometimes the desire section of a dream shows a sexual situation that could never actually happen in real life. Such plots can be used as fantasies to enhance lovemaking.

For example, a woman experiencing marital problems dreamed in the desire section that her husband started to make love to her and then changed into a gentler, more understanding, more attractive man. If, while making love with her husband, she fantasized that he instead was someone who possessed the desirable qualities she had dreamed about, she likely would find the sexuality with the husband more enjoyable.

It turns out that a desire section situation has the potential to affect subsequent sexual arousal even if it isn't about sex.

A man dreamed in the desire section:

I met a politician I had admired for a long time. He shook my hand in a friendly way. I looked in his eyes and could see he was sincere and virtuous.

If this actually happened, the dreamer would feel good because a desire of his had come true. And while experiencing that positive mood he spontaneously might wish for sexual relations--not with the politician but with his wife or any other appropriate sexual partner.

Here is another potential sexual catalyst. A woman dreamed this in the desire section:

The house we moved into needed some work done on it. At first I was disappointed with its appearance, but then I thought that I could easily fix it up.

Being willing to perform necessary tasks around the house could cause this woman to feel sexual desire. The happiness or pleasure she derived from that desirable work attitude could boost her spirits sufficiently to cause her to wish for lovemaking.

SEXUAL TURN-OFFS

If the nondesire section of a dream is about sex, it will be showing a scenario the inner self finds sexually undesirable. Of course, the inner self will have a good reason for classifying that situation as undesirable.

A man who was a beginning fencing student dreamed in the nondesire section of making love with an attractive female fencer he knew. That woman had declined to fence with him because he was a beginner and therefore wouldn't be a challenging opponent. In response, his dream was indicating that subconsciously he wasn't impressed with her beauty or fencing skills, but he valued more highly the willingness to help a beginner, and found her undesirable for lacking that trait.

If the dreamer attempted to make love with her while being influenced by that dream, he would be impotent. The involuntary nondesire he felt toward her would inhibit his sexual arousal.

Nondesire scenarios do not need to be about sex to have that inhibitory effect when they occur in real life.

A woman dreamed this in the desire and nondesire sections:

My children and I were in a barn that was warm and smelled of hay. We went toward the front entrance and found a room off of it where a man was living. He told us we couldn't go out that way and threatened us.

It is unlikely the woman could become sexually aroused while there were some threat either to her or to her children. That threat would be undesirable to her, and so would prevent her from feeling any sexual desire until she thought she and her children were safe. Dreams establish priorities in this way.

A man dreamed in the nondesire section of threatening to hit a smaller, weaker man who was a rival for a woman. In contrast to the previous example, there might not be any physical danger involved for the dreamer in this situation, but nevertheless it would be undesirable to his inner self if he were to act in that bullying manner. While feeling that nondesire, he would be impotent in any lovemaking situation.

Sometimes undesirable attitudes can cause impotence or frigidity.

A woman dreamed this in the nondesire section:

I saw a snake and at first was afraid it would bite me, but then I thought, "Oh, well, if it did bite me and I died, then all of my problems would be over."

If she voluntarily chose to devalue life in that way, she would become frigid due to the inner nondesire she felt.

Undesirable fantasies can have the same effect upon sexual functioning as undesirable attitudes. So during lovemaking, one should avoid fantasizing about the sorts of sexual situations that have appeared in one's nondesire sections or likely would appear in them.

What fantasies are those? Here is one of them. A man dreamed this in the nondesire section:

An unwashed bag lady offered herself to me. I began making love to her. She changed into an inflatable doll.

It would be foolish for that man to engage in any related fantasy while with a sexual partner. Suppose, for instance, that while making love with a woman he chose to imagine that she was not human but instead was an inflatable doll. He would lose his erection.

Of course, that single example did not begin to encompass all the different sorts of fantasy situations that would be undesirable. By observing the nondesire sections in your dreams, you will gain a more thorough understanding of what fantasies to avoid.

WHEN DREAM ENDINGS COME TRUE

When a hated situation from a dream occurs in real life and isn't satisfactorily resolved, the dreamer may become emotionally ill, develop a psychosomatic illness, and/or have a strong urge to act destructively. Fortunately, the vast majority of dream endings can be avoided. That is no accident, of course. The inner self has realized those situations are very bad, and accordingly wants the dreamer to feel an involuntary hatred for them as an incentive to avoid or escape them.

Let's look at examples of that constructive hatred.

An overweight woman dreamed at the end of a dream that she weighed "175 pounds of potato chips and ice cream." The woman's inner self was trying to get her to improve her eating habits by causing her to hate being overweight, especially as a result of eating junk food.

A gifted teenager dreamed at the end of a dream that he was living in a dull, ordinary environment. By causing him to hate that, the dream indirectly was pushing him to find gifted companions and stimulating interests.

After dreaming in the initial sections about being on a boat cruise with her family, a woman dreamed this in the hatred section:

I seem to remember Jack (my son) on a deck somewhere, standing and looking at us, but unable to get to where we were, even though he wanted to.

The dreamer reported that her son had been emotionally distant from the rest of the family, and also had displayed behavioral problems. So his physical separation in the dream was a symbol of his emotional and behavioral separation from the family, and the woman's hatred of those problems would motivate her to help her son overcome them.

At a time when I had become inactive with regard to working on this book, I dreamed in a hatred section the following alarming conversation:

A man said to me, "Do you want arthritis?"
"No," I answered.
"Then start writing," he said.

The inner self has that sort of power, but it doesn't abuse it. There were periods after that dream when I wrote so wretchedly that it was as if I hadn't written anything at all. Yet I'd been trying to write well during those times, and I haven't developed arthritis.

Here is a promise. If you pay attention to the goals shown in your dreams and try to bring those goals about, you'll be happier, more sexually passionate, and healthier.

But if you ignore your dreams, you'll be a gambler with the odds against you.

CHAPTER 5

FEELINGS IN THE DREAM PLOT

We have learned that a display of feeling by a dream figure will be either (a) genuine; or (b) opposite to emotional reality, and not truly felt. We also have learned a general rule about how to distinguish between the two: the emotional display (which I subsequently will call "emotionality") will be genuine if the emotional figure simultaneously speaks, and will be opposite to reality in the absence of that accompanying speech.

This seems simple enough, perhaps. Many people, though, find the concept of "insincere dream feelings opposite to reality" strange and confusing at their first introduction to it. Upon hearing that opposite emotions might be in the plot, some fall back on the opinion that dreams are mostly just vile nonsense.

In contrast, genuine feelings in the dream plot virtually always are easy to understand, even by those with no prior experience at analyzing dreams. This is no surprise, since the words help explain what the display of emotion is about, and the related situation clearly will be emotional in nature.

Look at how this is so.

GENUINE EMOTIONALITY

A man due to go on a business trip dreamed at the beginning of a dream that his girlfriend smiled gently and wished him a successful trip.

Both the words and the smile were communicating the same loving message.

(A mystery remains. Was that dream plot telepathic in nature? Was the love coming from the actual woman? Such questions are impossible to answer conclusively, but indeed it seems as if telepathy could have been involved. Nor is apparent telepathy in dreams a rare phenomenon, and we soon shall encounter another example of it.)

A woman dreamed this in the hatred section:

I turned to a bully who had tormented me all through grade school, hugged him, began crying, and said, "They told me to be afraid of you and I believed them."

The words explained why she felt sad, and the location of that scene in the hatred section shows she hated her unnecessary fear and the barriers it had created between him and her.

A man volunteered to water the plants and do other tasks at a friend's house while the friend was away on a vacation. The house was in the country and it took the man several hours to drive to it, do the work, and drive back. In a dream the man had that night, a dismayed figure appeared in the nondesire section. "You forgot to feed the fish," that person said.

A teenage girl who had some imaginary companions took an overdose of her parents' sleeping pills. She was rushed to the hospital and had her stomach pumped, and subsequently cried for a long time before falling asleep. She had a nurturing dream that night: she dreamed that Captain Amigo (one of her favorite imaginary friends) and other benign beings were looking at her lovingly. "We were really upset with you," Captain Amigo told her gently. His statement seemed to be implying she wouldn't try a suicide attempt again, and so was highly supportive.

The girl told me that the companions of Captain Amigo were displaying genuine love in their auras despite not speaking. This forms an exception to the usual condition that silent dream emotionality is opposite to reality, and it seems that "fairy godmothers" can bend the rules a bit when they appear in dream plots.

I saw silent genuine emotionality--and one or two fairy godmothers--in two of my own dreams.

At a time when I had begun eating too many candy bars and was starting to weigh too much, I dreamed in the nondesire section that someone offered a motherly-looking woman a candy bar. She smiled sweetly while turning her head away from it. That smile was an indirect way of asking that I follow her example, so I stopped eating candy bars and other unnecessary foods, and lost some weight in the next few weeks. I then dreamed in the desire section that a jovial fat man slapped my hand (as a football player might slap the hand of a teammate who has just scored a touchdown). It wasn't hard to figure out that my inner self was pleased with my improved eating habits.

But silent genuine emotionality won't be displayed only by fanciful creations of the dreamer's imagination. Some of that emotionality seems to come from real people, and may be telepathic in origin. For example, a man dreamed in his dream's ending of a woman who resembled his wife, except that in the dream she had a nightmarishly unhappy expression on her face. She looked at him without speaking.

Her image appeared in his hatred section, and the message simply may have been that he would hate for her to be as unhappy as the dream was depicting her. Yet did she genuinely feel that way? Also, did she have an emotional block about communicating her unhappiness to him during a conscious discussion? If so, her need to communicate her deep feeling may have enabled her to appear telepathically in his dream. An alternative, admittedly, is that her depiction in his dream was due to his inner sensitivity, with no telepathy involved.

It seems apparent from these examples that genuine emotionality in dreams offers a direct glimpse of the soul. Most emotionality in dreams, however, is the other type. For the sake of convenience, I shall refer to it as:

OPPOSITE EMOTIONALITY

It is usually the dreamer's image that displays opposite emotionality. This isn't surprising, since dreams primarily revolve around and reflect the dreamer. What might that emotionality reveal? All sorts of things, as it turns out.

HAPPINESS OPPOSITE TO REALITY

A girl whose boyfriend had moved away dreamed in the desire section of her dream of being cuddled up next to him and feeling secure and happy. Her image didn't speak, so that happy feeling wasn't a genuine one. She wanted to feel that way again (and to be with him again), and that is why she dreamed that scene in the desire section.

UNHAPPINESS OPPOSITE TO REALITY

This was a man's account of his first wet dream as a youth:

I was being chased by a gorilla through a forest. I saw a baby in a basket that was floating on a stream. I wanted to rescue the baby. I started to shinny across a log that lay in the stream. At this point the ejaculation occurred. Then there was no basket and no baby. I saw the gorilla in the woods and fired a water pistol at it. As I did so, I felt an overwhelming sadness.

He felt a very positive emotion (opposite to the sadness in the dream) about his maturing sexual development.

The dream also reveals he had a love of eluding a gorilla and a desire to rescue a baby. So although the plot might appear gloomy on the surface, it was showing an imaginative, adventurous adjustment.

It seems relevant to add that I knew the dreamer 20 years after he had that dream, and my impressions of him were of a happy, extroverted person who had a low threshold for boredom and was eager to engage in physically risky activities such as skydiving. In general, dreams such as that one which reflect basic personality inclinations also can be excellent predictors of future lifestyle.

A woman dreamed this in the last half of a dream:

I am somewhere that I do not want to be, like in a jail. There seems to be no way that I can obtain my freedom. I am crying.

In real life she had been experiencing a sense of being free, and felt happy as a consequence. The dream was reflecting this by showing how badly she'd feel if she were instead in jail.

It's natural to wonder at this point why it's necessary for dreams such as that one to distort things so. Why didn't her dream plot simply show her being happy about her freedom? Why did it have her image engage in the crying?

The answer is that crying was a valuable part of the dreamer's emotional repertoire, yet her ability to cry might diminish below a usable level if her life situation continued to be positive. Therefore her dream included the crying so she wouldn't lose that skill.

It turns out that dreams often exercise unused, valuable emotions via opposite emotionality.

THE EXERCISE OF UNUSED EMOTIONS

A single woman dreamed this in the love and desire sections of a dream after she'd had lunch with a pregnant friend who'd talked excitedly about her upcoming delivery:

I was with my family and had a baby. The baby was a girl with dark hair and big dark eyes and I loved her.

The pregnant woman's preoccupation with giving birth had caused the dreamer to realize at an inner level that she too wanted to experience the various dimensions of motherhood. So her dream contained the important feeling of love for a baby, and as a consequence she would find it easier to feel that same love again, including not only when she was pregnant or a mother but also when she was considering whether or not to have a child.

What other positive emotions besides motherly love get exercised in dreams? At times a yearning for one's optimal profession is included in the dream plot, as we now see. An actor fell upon hard times and had to take a job in a department store. His new job was much less creative and fulfilling, but one day--a month or so after he'd begun working there, with the vivid memories of acting beginning to fade--he enjoyed the trivial routines at work. That night he dreamed in the love section that he missed being an actor and experiencing the joy that it brings. At an inner level, he wanted to remain attached to acting rather than acquire positive feelings about his new job. That is why he dreamed that nostalgic feeling.

People experiencing marital difficulties sometimes dream of feeling romantic happiness in order to restore this "missing link" to their emotional capabilities. For example, a woman who felt neglected by her husband dreamed this in her nondesire section:

I went into a restaurant and saw an old boyfriend there. I was very happy to see him and sat and talked with him for a while. Then we went back to the hotel I was staying at. In the lounge there, we saw my husband, and he was with a woman I didn't know. He seemed very happy with this woman. I didn't even mind, because I was feeling so happy to be with my old boyfriend.

Both the dreamer and her husband felt happiness in the plot, and the conclusion is that neither had been feeling that emotion with each other. It seems the marriage was failing, and that may have been the reason the woman's dream exercised her ability to feel happiness with another man. Note, though, that she still wanted the marriage to succeed: the happy, carefree feelings she experienced in the dream occurred in the nondesire section, indicating it would be undesirable for her to be happy with the boyfriend rather than with her husband, and similarly undesirable for her not to be upset if she saw her husband with another woman.

Even a strongly negative emotion that appears at the end of a dream can become useful in the future.

A man dreamed that his son was injured in a traffic accident, and in the hatred section the dreamer felt rage. In real life his son was doing well after having moved away from home to be on his own, so the father's dream rage was inappropriate to what was actually happening. Yet if his son were injured or otherwise came to harm it might be natural for the father to feel that strong emotion, and therefore his dream exercised the rage even though he currently hated it. He would be able to access it if it ever became helpful to him in life's fluctuating circumstances.

One might suppose it's better for dreams to rehearse unused feelings of laughter than harsh feelings such as rage. That isn't the case, however. Dream laughter which is opposite emotionality won't guarantee future merriment, and its primary function is to imply present wretchedness.

LAUGHTER ABOUT LIFE'S MISERIES

A woman who was a writer and the mother of a 14-year-old girl reported this:

I dreamed at the beginning of a dream that my cousin Jack came to live with us. He was 14 years old and I was the same age I am now. He was wearing a cap like my daughter's.

She didn't remember any more of that dream but later that night dreamed:

I plan to announce that I have won the lottery. Everyone will then assume that what I have won is money. I will not tell them otherwise and will say that I want to share my good fortune. What I have won is Jack. I will give him away. Then I think this is a marvelous idea for a very funny story. I think it is hysterical. I laugh and laugh. I'm not sure which came first: the intention to write the story or the plan to rid myself of Jack by this means. Either way I am pleased with myself. Then I caution myself to make sure I am not plagiarizing this story from anyone. I say to myself, "Did I read this somewhere?"

The woman's laughter in the second dream indicates that something was bothering her in real life. What might that be? In the dream she laughed about a "marvelously funny story plot," and this implies that as a writer she had been having problems devising humorous plots. But the dream laughter was more specific than that: it was about the "story" of giving away Jack. Why did that theme result in her dream image expressing so much amusement?

The first dream showed Jack as the same age as the dreamer's daughter, and wearing a cap like the daughter's. Obviously, Jack was a symbol for the daughter, and with that in mind it becomes clear her intention in the second dream to give away Jack was really a disguised wish to give away her daughter. She didn't want to be a mother any longer. Such wishes are exceptionally painful, of course, and that is why she laughed so heartily in the dream.

What can be as miserable as that? The following is one such candidate. A woman dreamed in the nondesire section of her dream that she and a female friend laughed about the macho behaviors some men were displaying. That shared laughter indicates that in real life they both had been feeling unhappy about macho men.

As it happens, the love section of that dream is also worth reporting. In it, a man riding a mechanical bull was thrown from it. He then turned to a buddy and said, "Mama." The woman would love it if men could express a need for mothering--especially to each other--rather than always having to maintain a masculine image.

We have not come to an end of the intricacies of opposite emotionality.

UNSHARED EMOTIONALITY

Dreams can have one dream figure display opposite emotionality which another figure doesn't share, and by that contrast provide meaningful information.

An article had appeared in a newspaper about my original dream interpretation theories. The article suggested that readers with dreams they wanted interpreted according to those theories should write to me. A man called me instead. "You've made the greatest spiritual advance in two thousand years," he said. "I would like to meet you."

I wasn't eager to meet with the first-ever member of my fan club. I took his telephone number and told him I would contact him. Afterwards I worried I would hurt his feelings by not calling him--and I was considerably more worried that he would continue to call me.

A dream addressed those concerns that night. I dreamed in the hatred section:

I was with someone I recognized as being an inner-self figure. I was smiling about the situation involving my admirer, but the image of my inner self wasn't smiling and instead seemed calm. "Just forget it," that figure said.

My smile had been opposite emotionality and had implied the stress I consciously felt. The dream figure representing my inner self hadn't smiled, though, and in that way conveyed the view that the situation was harmless.

The absence of an opposite-emotionality smile, in other words, can be reassuring.

VARIETIES OF OPPOSITE EMOTIONALITY

Opposite emotionality is a much-used tool, and it often assumes diverse and creative forms within the dream plot.

A man dreamed the following in the nondesire section of his dream:

I was a political prisoner being led blindfolded across a platform, all the while having to clap in applause for the political figure who was seated nearby.

The applause was opposite emotionality, and was also part of an unpleasant experience in the dream. What was the overall meaning? The man reported that on the previous day he had pretended not to see a nearby acquaintance he hadn't wanted to talk to. His inner self disapproved, and the forced applause while blindfolded was a sarcastic means of signaling that his behavior of ignoring the acquaintance had not been a correct policy. (Yes, dreams can be sarcastic or otherwise punitive, although this doesn't happen often.)

A woman told me she dreamed this emotional attitude at the end of a dream:

I felt satisfied that the world was proceeding as it should in the light of the total existence of the universe and God.

"How do you feel about the world at the present time?" I asked her.

She shook her head. "I hope those poor Russian grandmothers survive the cold winter," she said with pangs in her voice. "I've been getting letters from relatives about the declining economy over there. There's no end in sight to their poverty."

So her conscious response was totally opposite to her optimistic attitude in the dream--and this wasn't surprising since that dream attitude was opposite emotionality.

I explained to her that the dream was rehearsing her ability to feel optimistic if world events took a change for the better. "The dream also was showing you'd hate to have that satisfied attitude at present," I added.

She shuddered. "Only ignorant people and ghouls would feel satisfied about what's happening."

I understood why her dream had rehearsed her ability to have a positive attitude.

A man dreamed in the love section about reading a comic book and finding scenes from his job in it. While talking with him, I learned that he frequently had to meet stressful deadlines at work and also sometimes had unpleasant interactions with his supervisor. So he would love it if his job instead could provide him with the same carefree enjoyment he associated with reading comic books.

I told him my interpretation and asked if there was any way he could learn to enjoy his job more, since his dream showed that wish.

"The dream has the answer," he said to me. "I can bring comic books to work and read them during my break."

Such a misunderstanding isn't surprising in response to opposite emotionality. I had to explain again to him the symbolic purpose of the comic book in his dream.

The example that follows includes a performance opposite to reality and a happiness at the end of the dream which also is unreal. After the love section (which is irrelevant to our current focus) had finished, a woman's dream continued:

I had a ten kilometer race to run--but somehow it was only three miles. Some friends of mine were there; they were going to run in it also. The race started and I was in the front because I was going to run it very fast. I was taking enormous strides and it seemed effortless. I ran and ran and then this woman was blocking my way by sitting in a chair with her legs across the route. I was frantic. "Move your legs," I shouted.
"The race is over; good luck," she said. I had won. I had run six-minute miles. I was very happy.

Her dream was a balanced one: the love and desire sections were showing wishes and fantasies, but the second half included a realistic orientation. She desired being in a ten kilometer race, except she wanted it to be only three miles long (about half that distance). She wanted friends of hers to run in that race also, so she viewed it as a sociable occasion. She would like it if she could take enormous strides and if her running could be effortless--but the woman who blocked the way was sitting in a chair, and that scenario implies the dreamer had sat too much (rather than exercising) prior to the race. Therefore, the enhanced running in the desire section was opposite to what the dreamer actually could expect. For that reason, it would be undesirable to feel a frantic need to move her legs to maneuver around obstacles, and she would hate to have her happiness dependent on running six-minute miles, since that speed evidently was an unrealistic goal for her when she wasn't in peak physical condition.

Note that the woman who blocked the way expressed a relaxed attitude about the outcome of the race. Her inner self was speaking through that figure, and inner-self figures in dreams are like that. They typically have high standards involving preparation and yet may not act concerned about actual performance.

THE INNER AWARENESS OF OTHER PEOPLE'S FEELINGS

We now proceed to examples in which dream figures other than the dreamer display the opposite emotionality. Such dream content can provide valuable--and surprising--information about other people's true feelings.

A woman who had been divorced by her husband after 30 years of marriage, because he had fallen in love with his secretary, reported the following dream:

I walked up to my husband--who was smiling and who all through the dream continued to smile--and I reached out to him, but he kept his hands at his side and never seemed to realize who I was. His secretary acted pretty much the same way. I began to beat her but she was smiling and completely relaxed as I continued to beat her.

"Why are both my ex-husband and the secretary smiling throughout the dream? I don't understand that part," the woman said to me with a troubled look on her face. "I wouldn't have thought either one of them would be happy about treating me the way they have." She was silent for a few seconds. "I realize," she added, "that the dream means I have violent impulses toward the secretary."

I explained the dream to her. The smiles her ex-husband and the secretary displayed were opposite emotionality, so the dream was implying that the two of them were feeling remorse. As for her violence, it had occurred only in the last half of the dream, and the true message regarding it was that she wouldn't want to beat the secretary, despite the provocation for doing so. "How we act in the nondesire and hatred sections of our dreams isn't how we'd genuinely want to act in real life," I said.

You might be curious whether her inner self, while creating that dream, had actually known that her ex-husband and the secretary were feeling remorse, or instead was only guessing. It probably knew the truth. As this next example illustrates, inner selves can be amazingly accurate in their assessments of other people's feelings.

I dreamed in the nondesire section of a dream that a man whom I'd recently met--a chess player whom I knew little about, and had last seen a week earlier--was sneering at me. I wondered about that dream after awaking from it, since the sneer apparently was opposite emotionality and yet I didn't know why the dream would include it. Was the dream message only that it would be undesirable if he were to act in that unpleasant way?

On the next day he called me up and asked me if I wanted to study some chess openings with him. Just a coincidence? No, my inner self had known he felt friendly.

How do inner selves obtain that sort of information? Is there any convincing explanation for it other than telepathy? This controversial topic will be resumed in the next chapter, and again the evidence will suggest that telepathy occurs in some dreams.

SYMBOLS FOR THE INNER SELF

Seemingly real people appearing in dreams--figures with flesh-and-blood counterparts--can be used as symbolic images of the dreamer's inner self. So in an instance such as the following when a "real" person in a dream displays opposite emotionality, one has to analyze whether it reflects that actual person's emotional reality or the dreamer's.

I dreamed in a nondesire section about the cashier at the cafeteria where, in everyday life, I usually had lunch. In the dream, she laughed and then told me to go to the gymnasium before eating. For several weeks before the dream I hadn't been exercising enough, and also had starting overeating, and the laughter revealed concern about those facts. But that cashier wasn't aware of them (and it seems most improbable that she would have felt any related pain had she known, since I was only a customer to her). Therefore, her image's laughter in the dream reflected concern I inwardly felt.

A Mixture of Emotionalities

At times, an inner self figure will display both opposite and genuine emotionality within the same sentiment in order to convey two separate messages. This should not prove confusing to the informed and resourceful interpreter (meaning you), and the following example shows how uncomplicated the messages can be.

A man dreamed in the love section that his younger brother walked toward him, smiling. The dreamer didn't have a younger brother but had always wanted one, and as opposite emotionality that smile implied his pain about the nonexistent, wished-for brother. Yet the dreamer reported that the smile had seemed real and had given him much pleasure. His inner self was helping him have a happy fantasy even while it revealed pain he felt.

The Nature of Most Silent Smiles in Dreams

That last example was an exception, and most silent smiles in dream plots are only grim.

A man reported about a dream ending:

I was in a gymnasium, exercising on some parallel bars. A figure that resembled me slipped from those bars and although he was still hanging on by his legs, he fell until his head almost struck the ground. The dream ended with him smiling.

The dreamer had been at various times a rodeo performer and a skydiver, and he'd had four concussions. That smile was expressing his inner concern that he not have any more, such as from hitting his head while exercising. The smile wasn't a happy one; there was nothing but anxiety underlying it.

THE CLARITY OF OPPOSITE EMOTIONALITY

Do you understand opposite emotionality thoroughly now? It shows an opposite of emotional reality, and also may be exercising an unused emotion, or providing an implication about a relationship, or carrying out any of its other valuable functions. It's a versatile tool dreams often use, and once understood it's as much a window into the soul as genuine emotionality.

CHAPTER 6

DREAM SPEECH

Dream speech is like a cross between an elementary reader and a calculus text. Some of it is very easy to understand, and some of it isn't.

Here is an example of the easy-to-understand variety. A woman dreamed the following at the end of a dream:

I suddenly knew I would leave the reality I was in to enter another, completely different one, and would not return to my old, familiar life. I cried out to a companion that I couldn't leave my sister this way and not come back. That companion replied that some things were inevitable. I said that maybe leaving her would be bearable, as I had talked to her by telephone this week, and we had each said, "I love you," so we had each communicated that truth. I waited in the cold and dark for the future to come.

The words contained no mysteries, and the hatred message was equally simple to interpret. The dreamer hated the necessity of leaving her sister and perhaps encountering a "cold and dark" future.

Despite the simplicity of that example, some dream speech will contain challenging complications. A dream figure may use words that seem to reveal thoughts or feelings but instead reflect behavior. Words with a symbolic meaning might be used, and before one can understand the communication one has to figure out the symbolism. Conversations can occur in which one side mumbles rather than speaking clearly. Two inner-self figures might be shown arguing about the best course for the dreamer to follow. We shall see examples of all of the above in this chapter, plus other creative but potentially confusing uses of language in the dream plot.

All such complexity in dream content is necessary when it occurs; some dream messages are about abstract or otherwise complicated topics and would be impossible to convey via a simple dream plot. The conscious process of analyzing those messages needn't prove difficult, though. Dreams don't deliberately try to make things hard for the interpreter, and there are shortcuts based on understanding that lead directly to the meaning.

Here is one such shortcut (and it may seem intuitively obvious, and yet no previous dream interpreter ever caught a clear glimpse of it and attempted to define it using supporting examples): **when the dreamer's image speaks, the words reflect a dominant aspect of the conscious self; in contrast, words by any other dream figure may be revealing an inner orientation which generates conscious opposition, although speech by other dream figures can have a variety of roles and won't always reflect "suppressed" aspects of the psyche.**

Looking at the previous dream with this in mind, one concludes that the dreamer was expressing sentiments which may have originated deep within her but which were fully shared or experienced by her conscious self. Consequently, her image spoke those words.

In this next example, however, someone other than the dreamer's image had to be the speaker. A man with macho tendencies was experiencing problems, and one night he dreamed in the hatred section of his dream that someone suggested to him, "Cry." Crying evidently would be beneficial, but he consciously was opposed to that recourse. Therefore, his own image couldn't suggest it.

Partly because of such self-imposed barriers to inner emotions, the conscious individual usually is moody, variable, and otherwise complex. (Do you fit that description? Do you know anyone else who does?) The words the dreamer's image speaks, nevertheless, are able to reflect the conscious self accurately. Nor does that accuracy seem to diminish when the dreamer becomes neurotic or even psychotic.

THE DREAMER SPEAKS

For practical reasons, we now must add a new word to our vocabulary: "dreamerspeech." It refers to words spoken by the dreamer's image, but not to words spoken by any other dream figure.

Among its other roles, dreamerspeech can allow the dreamer to express feelings which might be frowned upon by society. In illustration, a pregnant woman dreamed that she said in a dream ending, "I don't want to be pregnant." She reported that she had been feeling unhappy about the discomfort and limitations associated with her pregnancy, and admitted that what she said in the dream was true. She also said that it was beneficial to see her dream image speak those honest words.

Dreamerspeech can help the dreamer make happy statements as well: a woman who enjoyed dancing dreamed in the desire section that she said, "Dancing is a means of expressing my true self, and it helps me become a more genuine person." Perhaps at a nonverbal level she'd known that all along, yet she said that until dreaming those words she hadn't fully understood dancing's value to her.

In this next dream, the dreamerspeech enabled the dreamer to express an inner state which differed significantly from her public role. A woman had visited some people she scarcely knew in order to view Halley's comet, and all of the others had acted excited about what they saw and so she did also. Overall, her experiences hadn't been satisfying to her, and that night she dreamed in the love section:

I was at my friend Jack's house. He was there with his wife and some others. We were there to look at Halley's comet. We went outside to the platform where he had his telescope. It was warm outside. The people there liked me and wanted me to stay. I saw the comet in the sky and I asked Jack, "Is that it? Is that the comet?" It was, and it was very impressive.

The dream shows that she would have loved for the viewing to have occurred at her friend's house, and she would have loved for the people in that imagined setting to value her company. Also, she would have loved for the comet to be impressive, but her dreamerspeech reflected a relatively neutral mood about what she saw through the telescope. So those words her dream image spoke in the love section depicted a contrast to her conforming behavior at the party she'd attended, and the implication is that she would have loved being herself at that party.

THE SURPRISES OF DREAMERSPEECH

Sometimes dreamerspeech occurs in a surprising location in relation to the message being spoken.

An engineer dreamed in the nondesire section that he said, "I can view engineering problems from both a macroscopic and a microscopic perspective." He was talking about a talent of his, so why did he speak those words in his dream's nondesire section? There was a logical explanation. At the time of the dream he was unemployed and was feeling discouraged about finding an employer who would recognize and value his engineering aptitude. The location of his words reflected that discouragement. (But if he'd been more discouraged than he was, he might have spoken them in the hatred section rather than in the nondesire section. Generally, the bleakest points of view and worst situations will show up in dream endings rather than in late-middle locations.)

The most surprising aspect of dreamerspeech, though, usually is the words themselves rather than their location. As noted, those words reflect a feature of the conscious self, yet consciousness tends to be at least partly ignorant of its true nature. So dreamerspeech can tell unexpected secrets.

I had a friendly neighbor who owned a playful dog. Its name was "Wishbone" and I consciously thought of it by that name. One rainy day it jumped on me and got mud on my clothes. That night I dreamed in the hatred section that I said to it, "Leave me alone, dog." My dream self was understandably angry about the muddy clothes and was showing that anger partly by not addressing the dog by its cute name. Strange as it might seem, however, I hadn't consciously realized I felt that negative emotion. It was there, but I had managed to ignore it because of my positive feelings toward my neighbor. Therefore, my words in the dream surprised me.

Human consciousness selectively concentrates on some things and ignores others, and dreams will always contain such surprises.

THE MEANING OF "GIBBERISH"

Dreamerspeech can include the use of words that aren't in any dictionary. As one example, I dreamed in a hatred section that golden objects were being thrown at me, and in response I said, "Pyongyongyong."

What on earth did that strange utterance mean? A recent memory--and dream pattern analysis--helped me understand it. I had gone shopping for a Christmas gift for friends, and had wandered through a number of stores looking for the right gift but not finding it. Finally, I spotted an ornament with an oriental design and bought it. My "Pyong" speech, with the oriental tinge to the sounds, depicted my decision to buy that ornament. Nor did I hate that purchase. What I had hated had been the frustrating search, symbolized in the hatred section by the golden objects being thrown at me.

(But I didn't consciously realize any of this until after I'd had that dream and analyzed it.)

THE POSSIBLE FUTURE SELF

Dreamerspeech usually reflects the conscious self which exists at the time of the dream, and all of the examples in this chapter up to now have done so. Once in a while, though, dreamerspeech will reveal a change within the dreamer which might occur in the future. The inner self is sufficiently in touch with trends or possibilities within the conscious self to make such predictions.

As you might suppose, if that different self appears in a love or desire section, the related message is that the change is a positive one, while the opposite is true for any changed future self appearing in a nondesire or hatred section.

Three examples follow of dreamerspeech about a possible future self.
All are from my own dreams, since it's a difficult and unsure process to
distinguish present self versus future self in other people's dreamerspeech.

(1) My girlfriend's two-year-old daughter liked to talk with me when
I'd call from out of town, but she usually would have to gather her
thoughts before she knew what to say. "You know what?" she'd happily
ask when her mother put her on the telephone.

"What?" I'd say.

She'd think again for a few seconds. "You know what?" she'd ask
again.

"What?"

Another pause. "You know what?"

At some point, of course, she'd either think of something else to say or
her mother would intervene out of consideration for my telephone bill.

One evening I called to say that I couldn't visit them that weekend due
to an unavoidable circumstance. That night I dreamed in the love section
that I was speaking on the telephone. "You know what? You know what?
You know what?" my dream image said.

My dream words, an imitation of the child's sociable behavior, were
showing me as I could become. The related message was that I would love
acting sociably on the telephone with the woman and her child, as opposed
to canceling a visit to them.

(There is a sequel which shows the constructive consistency dreams
can display. A year later I abruptly decided to end my relationship with the
child's mother. I told myself I'd inform the woman the next morning that
the trips to visit them were becoming too difficult and money was a
problem, and logic seemed to dictate that we break up. That night I
dreamed in a vivid nondesire section that the child said to me, "I feel
betrayed." My inner self had seen my intention, didn't like it, and had
responded with its opposing perspective. So I didn't have that "logical"
talk the next day, and continued to visit the two of them.)

(2) One night I dreamed in the desire section that I said, "I can hear the
bells." Awake, I somehow knew those bells were the ones in a poem by
Edgar Allan Poe: they had rung to announce major changes such as a

wedding or a childbirth. Were any such changes likely in my life? Not at that time, but the possibilities for such change existed, and it would be desirable if I were to become more aware of them.

On the evening before that dream, I had spent several hours studying chess. I thought about that, and saw that I'd been spending immense amounts of time studying for chess tournaments and competing in them, and meanwhile other aspects of life were passing me by. I decided it would be best to have new interests and experiences, and as well to change my personality to some extent. (Typically, dedicated chess players tend to be introverts.) All in all, those symbolic bells were worth hearing, even though they might require considerable efforts on my part to respond appropriately to them.

(3) A few months after I had been fired from a psychology position which involved much paperwork, I dreamed in the nondesire section of a dream that I was back at work there. In that plot, I looked at stacks of psychology reports on my desk and said, "Being fired from that job was the worst thing that has ever happened to me."

I hadn't been missing that job, so my dream words were showing a possible future attitude, and the location of those words in the nondesire section indicated that such an attitude would be undesirable. Why would it be undesirable? The reports stacked on the desk were a clue. After I had been fired, I'd had more time to talk with people about their dreams, and had managed to collect over a hundred dreams to use in this book. Those dreams were stacked on my real-life desk, and it became apparent the dream was asking me to compare the value of the psychology reports I would have written at that lost job with the value of the dreams I instead had acquired. It wasn't hard to figure out that the dreams were more valuable, and that I indirectly was being encouraged via that nondesire plot to write this book.

(It seemed no disgrace to be fired from that position. My supervisor had said that children who cried shouldn't receive attention from adults until they stopped, and I had felt obliged to disagree with him. Things started going downhill. Additionally, he was fond of stating that he liked Darth Vader's ways of responding to people, and he looked at me strangely after I mentioned I was a Luke Skywalker fan. Altogether, he seemed quite

certain that we weren't on the same wavelengths at all. My dreams
predicted the final outcome, and were supportive when it happened.)

SYMBOLIC LANGUAGE

Symbolic dream language often reflects a complex situation. A
teenage boy was pestered by a girl who sometimes would hit or kick him
to get his attention. One night he dreamed in the nondesire section that a
mouse was biting him, on a spot where the girl had kicked him, and he
said, still in nondesire, "I hate that little mouse!"

Subtle information was being conveyed in that plot. The fact that the
dreamer symbolically spoke about hating a mouse rather than the girl
suggests that he didn't hate her when she wasn't being a violent "animal."
Also, he dreamed about the mouse biting him in his dream's nondesire
section rather than in the hatred section, so this indicates her playful
physical aggressiveness toward him was merely undesirable to his inner
self, despite his conscious tendency to hate that behavior.

It is useful to add that her behavior soon improved--with a few slip-
ups--and it wasn't too long before he began dreaming about her in the first
half of his dreams. That symbolic dreamerspeech was about an important
topic with the capacity to evoke more than one emotion in him.

FEEDBACK TO DREAMERSPEECH

The conscious self sometimes gets off the right tracks, and at such
times a dream might include dreamerspeech reflecting that
"dysfunctionality" in a plot which also points out a correct adaptation. The
dream's corrective guidance can be delivered by a wise inner-self figure
during a conversation with the dreamer, as we shall see later in this
chapter. But dreams also can use nonverbal means to accomplish that same
communicative goal.

For example, a man who had become discouraged about not having a
girlfriend dreamed this in a nondesire section:

I said, "I'll never find a woman who's on my wavelengths." Then I saw a succession of images of attractive women.

What was undesirable was the conscious attitude shown in his words; the attractive women in his dream were desirable to him. The dream was using those images of the women as a reassurance that he could indeed find someone "on his wavelengths," and so was contradicting his conscious pessimism.

REFLECTIONS OF BEHAVIOR

Since the primary function of dreamerspeech is to define the conscious self, sometimes those words will reflect the dreamer's self-defining conscious behavior. Perhaps on those occasions the dreamerspeech might seem strange or even incomprehensible--until one realizes that the words should be evaluated in relation to conscious actions rather than to conscious thoughts or feelings.

A man who had spent an evening watching television dreamed that night in the first half of a dream that he was at a party, and then, in the nondesire section, dreamed this:

Suddenly I seemed to be the life of the party, cutting up and cracking jokes, none of which I remember. Then I approached a man who had been doing a lot of talking, and, holding an empty wine glass up to him as if it were a microphone, said, "Here, say something to the network."

The dreamer's joking in the dream hadn't involved actual words, and therefore was opposite emotionality. It indicated he had felt none of that merriment while watching television. The other person in the dream was a symbol for the dreamer, and was shown as being talkative in order to indicate the dreamer's gregarious inner nature. The dreamerspeech to that symbol of himself about saying something to the "network" was reflecting his conscious behavior of ignoring and frustrating his sociable inclinations by watching television. That self-restrictive behavior was undesirable, as shown by its location in the nondesire section.

Here's another, simpler example. I had been trying to stick to a diet, but slipped off it one evening, eating everything in sight. After the food was gone, I consciously resolved not to do that again, but nevertheless dreamed that night in a nondesire section that I said, "Eat it all up." The words were an accurate portrait of myself, drawn from my undesirable behavior.

VOCALIZATIONS SUCH AS HOWLS AND SCREAMS

Some dreamerspeech won't involve any words at all, even made-up ones.

A hunter reported he had dreamed:

I was deer hunting in a wooded hollow similar to where I killed a deer several years ago. I heard a sound on the ridge at the far side of the hollow. I looked intently through the brush and saw a pack of large wolves. They were gaunt and looked hungry. The wolves hesitated at the edge of the hollow. I knew they were looking for a path of entry to it. Suddenly I realized I had no weapon. How could I have gone hunting without a rifle? The wolves started in my direction. What could I do to defend myself? As quick as a flash, I knew that if I howled like a wolf they would respect my territory. I howled. The wolves made a right angle turn. My wife shook me awake. "What in the world is the matter with you? Howling like a wolf!"

Analysis of the dream howl indicates it was showing the pain the dreamer would feel if he weren't a hunter, and at the same time was exercising the dreamer's ability to feel kinship with wolves. Opposite emotionality has such dual functions, and it becomes apparent that's what the howl was.

A woman dreamed this in the nondesire section of her dream:

Men weren't paying any attention to me, and I got very angry and shouted that I'd go outside topless and scream. Outside, no one looked at me, and when I tried to scream it came out of my throat as just a low, melodious tone.

A melodious attempt at a scream in the dream plot is a complex expression of feeling--and that alone can tell us it is opposite emotionality, since genuine emotionality will seem natural and contextually uncomplicated. As opposite emotionality, the melodious scream was opposite to a reality in which something frustrating was causing the dreamer to feel "unmelodious." What might that be? The fact that her dream self screamed while she was topless and being ignored suggests that the problem involved unfulfilled sexuality, including not being flirted with or considered sexy by men. Also, if she customarily uttered melodious sounds when experiencing orgasm, then a melodious tone in her dream would be reflecting that lack of sexual satisfaction.

The principal lesson for us from these two examples isn't that people scream in their dreams when they have unsatisfied sexual longings or howl when they want to be hunting. Rather, it is that dreamerspeech which utters primitive or animal sounds is opposite emotionality, and should be analyzed as such.

ATTEMPTED ESCAPES FROM REALITY

Dreamerspeech must be versatile enough to reflect the conscious self in all the different ways it can evolve and change. One of those potential changes, of course, is insanity. How would this be shown? A possible depiction of it follows.

A man whose wife had recently died dreamed:

My wife walked up to me at a social gathering. I put my arms around her and hugged her. Then I turned to some people who were standing nearby and said, "I knew she would come back." I felt happy.

Did his dreamerspeech mean he truly believed his wife would return from the grave? The love and desire sections showed her return, and those wishes might seem an additional indication he had that insane belief about her. Or his words might instead be depicting his possible future self, and thereby reveal a fragile prevailing sanity.

Either possibility would be bleak--but there is another interpretation which can be given to his dreamerspeech, and although it would indicate maladjustment it wouldn't necessarily imply an actual or latent psychosis. Perhaps his speech wasn't reflecting a belief but instead his behavior. If, while mourning his wife, he had been restricting his social contacts with people who could take her place or at least offer some measure of solace or comfort to him, then he would have been acting as though she would return. That would not be a satisfactory adjustment, of course. His dreamerspeech may have been defining his behavior for him so that he would have a better chance of understanding its undesirable nature and realizing he should change.

The happiness in the hatred section was opposite emotionality and showed that the dreamer felt unhappy in real life. The context provided by the dreamerspeech helps us understand the dream pattern message. It seems apparent he would have hated feeling happy about any socially reclusive behavior he engaged in.

In the next dream, the dreamerspeech reflected an abnormal state of mind which was a first step toward escaping from reality. It also illustrates a complication in the use of language which we haven't previously examined: unspoken but attempted speech.

I had been intending to play in a regional chess tournament several hundred miles away. Friends of mine would be there, and also I would enjoy competing for the substantial prizes being offered. But circumstances interfered, and I didn't go to the tournament. Several months afterwards, in a dream's hatred section, I wanted to talk about traveling to the chess tournament in time to play in it, but was unable to speak.

The attempted speech was about an impossible wish, and the fact that I had tried to speak implies I wanted to ignore reality. I was still sane, though, and so my dream self couldn't utter those words. The assumption is that if the unfulfilled wish had been stronger it could have driven me insane. (Fortunately, chess tournaments aren't worth losing one's sanity over.)

We have seen that dreamerspeech helps the dreamer understand his or her conscious self. Suppose, though, that the inner self wants to use words in a dream to provide a message about a relationship. How can it best do that? It turns out another form of dream speech tends to be better suited for that purpose.

A FAMILIAR PERSON SPEAKS

If the dream image of someone the dreamer knows in everyday life is depicted speaking in a usual role, then the purpose is to reveal how the dreamer feels toward that person in that role. Some dreams, in fact, might contain several such depictions. For example, a recovering alcoholic dreamed the following:

I'm helping other men I know load luggage in preparation for a trip. I'm standing at the rear of a car loading a suitcase, when one of my buddies sets a can of beer on the bumper and says, "Here is a cold one for you." Without thinking, I pick it up and guzzle about half of it down. Then I look to my left, and my youngest son is standing there and he says, "What are you doing?"
"Oh, my god, I forgot. I don't drink anymore," I say, and throw away the rest of the beer in disgust.

The friend and the son in that dream were displaying typical roles, and it's clear what the dreamer's related feelings were. He wanted his friend to offer him a beer, and he found it undesirable for his son to remind him he was drinking.

There is more to analyze: the hatred section portrays some ambivalence within the dreamer about drinking. His dream words indicate he consciously was trying to avoid alcohol, but he also would hate throwing the beer away. It seems difficult for the dreamer to avoid alcohol altogether, and perhaps total abstention isn't the best policy for him.

Are words by a familiar figure (or figures) always as understandable as in that previous example? No, but inevitably there will be a good reason for the more complex language usage. Consider the following, for example. A youth who had broken up with his girlfriend because his parents didn't like her dreamed in the nondesire section of his dream that she said, "My parents still miss her."

Those words seem confusing when uttered by her image, yet their meaning would be apparent if he instead had spoken them in the dream. They were expressing his inner wish that his parents had liked her all along. In that wishful scenario, it would be easy to resume the relationship with her. Clearly, he hadn't wanted to end the relationship, and had been mourning its absence.

Why did his girlfriend's image rather than his own speak those words? You may remember the general rule introduced at the beginning of this chapter: the words spoken by the dreamer's image reflect the conscious self, but words by someone other than the dreamer may be depicting an orientation which generates conscious opposition. That rule applies here. The dreamer had been conforming in his conscious thoughts and sentiments to the standards of his parents, and so the dream had to use his girlfriend's image rather than his own to express the regret he felt involving her. Rather a grim example of how we can internalize other people's values at the cost of our own!

Anxiety rather than a wish can underlie the words of someone familiar. A woman sometimes witnessed a man severely scold his son, and one night she dreamed in her nondesire section that the boy said, "He's giving me brain damage." Those words were beyond the boy's verbal capabilities, and the dream wasn't implying he actually would speak them. The purpose instead was to show the woman's inner concern that the father was harming his son.

The father didn't actually beat the boy, so that statement about brain damage was symbolic. It symbolized the likelihood that the boy was developing emotional and personality problems due to the scoldings. Why was that symbolism used? Probably because it was a vividly dramatic way to express the dreamer's anxiety.

Dreams are at their best when they do more than just inform about problems, and we now see an instance in which a familiar person's words offered a healing perspective. A woman who had been mourning the death of a close friend dreamed this:

I went to view my friend's body, which was in my grandmother's living room rather than at the funeral parlor. A number of people came by to pay their last respects. I waited until I was alone before going up to view the body. I was crying. Suddenly the corpse turned its head, winked at me, and said, "Don't be sad, I'm not really dead."

This is what the words meant to the dreamer: that she still had her happy memories of her friend. Her inner self would have hated it (in a kindly sort of way) if she weren't receptive to that healing message.

It is interesting to find out why, as the dream began, her friend's body was in her grandmother's living room. The dreamer said she had spent many happy hours as a child in that living room, so she had associations of love for it. Consequently, seeing the body in that location enhanced the love she felt about her memories of her friend.

The other messages in that dream plot also are healthy ones. It was desirable to her that people come by to pay their last respects to the dead woman. Her crying was opposite emotionality (since she didn't simultaneously speak), and showed she was beginning to experience a lessening of grief as she carried on in everyday life. She inwardly welcomed that progression away from mourning, since the related nondesire message was that it was undesirable to cry, especially while alone.

What sorts of negative statements do familiar people make in dreams? One example is sufficient. A woman dreamed in the hatred section that her husband said to her, "I'm no longer interested in sleeping with you." That was not a comforting thing to hear his image say.

Regarding those words, the question could be asked: did her husband feel the same way in real life? Of course, the answer wouldn't matter to us as uninvolved observers of that dream--except it touches upon a mysterious phenomenon.

THE QUESTION OF DREAM TELEPATHY

When a familiar dream character speaks directly to the dreamer, that communication can seem to be telepathic in origin. But did the telepathy actually occur?

Sometimes the answer is no. The inner self instead is showing a wished-for conversation.

I had received a bad final evaluation from a supervisor in a psychology position. I had asked him to change it, but he apparently was not going to do so. Then I had a dream in which he appeared in my desire section. "I'll give you a better evaluation," he said. After I awakened I felt relieved, since I thought he had spoken telepathically to me in that dream. In real life, though, my evaluation was never changed. So what I had assumed was telepathy was merely a wish of mine that his dream image speak those words.

Here is a similar misconception. I had begun attending a club's meetings. One evening I couldn't attend, and that night I dreamed in the desire section that one of the women in the club--someone I particularly liked--said, "Where were you last night, Dan?" Thinking about that after awakening, I assumed she had missed me, and therefore had appeared telepathically in the dream to ask about my absence. I subsequently learned, though, that she hadn't been at the meeting either. Therefore, those words from her image weren't telepathic, and instead were showing my inner wish that they were.

Despite these two examples, it's wrong to conclude that any dream which is seemingly telepathic can be explained as being only a wish. Some dreams would seem to strain all the laws of logic and probability if they don't indeed contain telepathy.

Here is one of them, and it provides the clearest evidence for dream telepathy that I could find. One night a widow dreamed that her dead husband appeared to her with his arms outstretched as if to hug her, and he had tears in his eyes. Half an hour after that dream, the telephone rang. A relative told her that her parents had been killed during the previous hour in an automobile accident. But her dream had already seemed to know about that tragedy.

(Was the dream proof that her husband's spirit existed in an afterlife? Not entirely. It's possible that her dream had only used his image in that role to provide a nurturing spiritual fantasy. Admittedly, though, it can be hard not to believe that such dreams as that one do provide glimpses of an afterlife.)

The dreams which follow also are potential examples of telepathic communication within the dream plot.

A man dreamed in the last half of a dream:

My ex-wife crouched down like a cat and hissed at me. "Diminish yourself," she said.

Afterwards the dreamer didn't know what that dream meant, and came to me for an explanation.

"Since your ex-wife's words appear in the hatred section, they presumably express hostility," I said. "Perhaps they are a pretentious way of telling someone to get lost."

He nodded, looking sad. "That's her, all right." His curiosity about that dream ended--but I was left wondering. Had that dream appearance by his ex-wife's image been telepathic? Or was the dream merely depicting a scenario involving her that he wouldn't like, without necessarily indicating what she actually felt toward him?

I concluded she had appeared telepathically in his dream. Her hiss in nondesire convinced me of that. The hiss had to be genuine (rather than opposite emotionality), since it fit in so well with the words she spoke. Nor did that hiss presumably come from his inner self (speaking through her image), since inner-self communications will be constructive in nature, even if they express anger, and there seemed nothing constructive about the hiss. Therefore, the genuineness was coming from the actual woman, and his dream was providing her with the opportunity to express herself freely to him.

At one time in my life I worked on a ranch, and had a furnished room there. One night I dreamed about the owner's wife in the nondesire section. "You've been letting your bedspread droop on the floor," she said in an intensely annoyed voice. The next day she told me, with a trace of that same annoyance, that I had been letting my bedspread droop onto the floor and it would get dirty there.

Her appearance in my dream seemed telepathic beyond any doubt, not only because of the identical nature of her dream statement and her subsequent words to me in real life, but also because until that dream I had never given much (if any) thought to the cleanliness of bedspreads. It seemed highly improbable that my inner self would suddenly get onto that wavelength if telepathy weren't the cause.

Ten years after high school, I dreamed in the desire section that I was talking with a girl I'd known back then. "Would you like to come to my apartment tonight?" I asked her.

"No, because I'm pregnant with my fourth child," her image answered.

In analyzing that unusual conversation, I guessed I had dreamed it for the following reasons. The woman's inner self had felt nostalgia for her high school days and had wanted to communicate with a friend from that period. So she contacted my sleeping self, and together our inner minds arranged that dialogue. By asking her to come to my apartment, I was helping her re-experience the popularity and freedom she had enjoyed in high school. By telling me about her pregnancy, she was declining my invitation in a tactful way.

(Unfortunately, I didn't know her address, and had no way to check whether she was indeed pregnant with her fourth child.)

One night a chess player appeared in the desire section of my dream. "I'm going to start studying the King's Gambit," he told me excitedly, referring to a chess opening which, although risky, can offer good chances to win, especially against an unprepared opponent. Several weeks later, I met him at a chess tournament, and he told me that he had begun studying the King's Gambit. Just a coincidence? I didn't think so.

In these examples of potential telepathy, a familiar person has spoken with the dreamer. I have no examples in which the dreamer speaks telepathically to someone else. The reason is simple. If someone speaks in his or her own dream, that communication won't be telepathic. One has to speak in another person's dream for telepathy to occur. As I personally learned, though, the speaker will have no subsequent memory of that "guest appearance."

I became sick one evening. I felt miserable. The next morning my girlfriend called me. "I had a dream last night," she said. "In it you told me you were sick." She imitated my dream voice for me. "I'm sick," she moaned, sounding as if she were 90 years old and dying. "I'm sick," she repeated, sounding even more ancient and feeble. She then stopped imitating me in order to laugh.

I had no memory of having talked to her in any of my dreams that previous night.

AN UNFAMILIAR FIGURE SPEAKS

Figures created by the unconscious self to appear in our dreams and speak to us can have all the wisdom and benevolence of fairy godmothers. The guidance and love they convey can have a dramatic and lasting influence.

AN INNER FIGURE SPEAKS TO THE DREAMER

A beautiful woman smiled at me in the love section of one of my dreams. "I saw you'd work on your dream book today," she said. (So of course I did, and additionally resolved never to disappoint her in my writing efforts.)

At a time when I'd been neglecting some important opportunities in my life, a sincere, earnest man asked me in the love section of a dream, "Did you hear my prayer?" It wasn't necessary for him to specify what his prayer was about, since I knew what it referred to.

After I'd begun eating junk food, a man who looked like an archetypal older brother, both affectionate and tough, appeared in the desire section of my dream. "You don't need that shit," he said to me.

Why did he speak in the desire section, since his message was about a situation in which I wasn't acting desirably? The answer is that my inner self believed I would follow that guidance. If I consciously had barriers against stopping the unhealthy eating, those words would have been spoken in the nondesire or hatred section instead, and the speaker would have appeared angry or upset.

In fact, here is an instance in which an inner figure was displeased. I was planning to write a foolish letter to a colleague. A man's image appeared in the nondesire section of my dream to tell me not to write that letter, and he spoke wearily and patiently, as one might speak to a dull-witted, troublesome child.

A guiding, inner-self figure won't always be immediately recognizable as such, and might instead change to that identity as the dream plot unfolds.

I visited a professional person whose office was in a high-crime neighborhood. Subsequently, I dreamed the following in a dream's nondesire section:

Two would-be muggers were trying to break into my car while I was inside it. One of those men made several such attempts, and then backed away, saying, "I don't want to drive it." As he departed, I thought about obtaining a knife and getting revenge against such criminals.

Those words spoken by the "mugger" were coming from my inner self, which didn't want me to drive in that dangerous neighborhood. Before speaking those alarmed words, however, that figure acted as he did in order to show me what could happen in such neighborhoods.

My thought in that nondesire section was being identified as an undesirable one, of course. The related message was that if I were to come into contact with criminals, it would be better to escape with my skin intact than to fight any of them because of a foolish wish for revenge.

The prelude to this next example is that I did poorly in a chess tournament and afterwards felt discouraged. That night I dreamed in a nondesire section:

A woman chessmaster was looking for strong opponents so that she could keep in practice. I thought that I shouldn't play her as I wouldn't be able to give her the competition she needed. She then

turned to me and said encouragingly, "Oh, it's terrible to think that. You play well."

So at that point of the dream she changed into someone who was warm and reassuring. The situation might seem trivial--a chess player's poor performance--but that inner figure was responding to the accompanying pain, which was real.

As we've seen, the appearance and personality of a dream figure can contribute much to the overall message. Yet some communications to the dreamer are relatively impersonal, and don't require an individuality on the part of the speaker.

On one occasion I noticed I had plaque on my teeth and was surprised, since I had been brushing them regularly. In a subsequent dream, an indistinct person in the desire section said to me, "Brush your teeth more slowly." That dental advice wouldn't have been enhanced by the vivid subtleties a dream face can convey.

WHEN THE DREAMER RESISTS A MESSAGE

If a dream figure has to tell a message which the dreamer doesn't want to hear, that figure might not speak directly to the dreamer.

For example, a woman on welfare dreamed one night in the nondesire section of her dream that a man told her sister (who was as poor as the dreamer) not to buy expensive foods. The dreamer often spent more than she should on food, and the words were intended for her. But she consciously believed her children should have the best food available to eat regardless of its price, and so that practical dream message was spoken to her sister's image rather than to her. In the ordinary course of events, the dreamer might spontaneously realize those words were meant for her when everyday realities helped her realize the value of that sort of economizing. (I interrupted that natural process by interpreting the dream message for her, and in response she talked bitterly about the economic injustices that prevail.)

If a figure in a dream of yours either speaks to another person than you
or addresses his or her words to no one in particular, ask yourself if you
have a conscious resistance to the message.

UNFAMILIAR HUMAN FIGURES SPEAK

Not all of the unfamiliar people who speak in our dreams will be
inner-self figures with "fairy godmother" messages. Some of those dream
characters instead will represent persons we might meet in the everyday
world, and their words will be appropriate to such roles.

This was the first half of a woman's dream:

**Grandmother and I were walking down a street that turned out to be
a dead end. Just as we got to the end, we discovered it. A nice man was
there and we asked permission to cross by the little pond in his yard
and go through to the next street. He said we could and then helped us
across. I commented on how clear and clean the pond was. He was
pleased. Then he showed us his baby seal. I asked if I could pet it. "Of
course," he said, and I began petting it and playing with it. Then his
wife began talking to me. It wasn't clear what she was saying, but she
continued to speak to me. The seal became a baby.**

The man's words and accompanying behavior show the dreamer's wish
that a property owner would be permissive and kindly to her while she was
going for a walk in a residential area.

Other aspects of that dream are worth attention.

The wife's verbal behavior might seem confusing. What is the value of
dream speech that doesn't include specific words? But a moment's
reflection clears up this puzzle for us. In a friendly environment such as
the one shown in the dream, the dreamer desires being spoken to, and it
wouldn't necessarily matter what the conversation was about. Instead, the
other person's sociability would be the important aspect.

That desire section shows the dreamer has a wish to play with a cute,
cuddly animal such as a seal. But then that seal is transformed into a
human baby. The dreamer's wish to interact with a pet animal evidently is

a sublimation of her stronger desire to respond maternally to a child. Her inner self saw this second desire, of course, and constructed the dream to help her get in touch with that maternal urge.

A woman dreamed this in the desire section:

My date was waiting at the door to the party. He said, "The tuxedos are all black now." And indeed all the men were wearing black, ruffled shirts.

That male figure's statement doesn't convey the sort of adaptive guidance that we have seen inner-self figures express. Instead, those words simply reflect the dreamer's taste in fashionable clothing.

What types of conversations might two (or more) dream figures have? Would they chat about the weather? They generally have more personal topics to talk about, as it turns out.

CONVERSATIONS

The usual participants in a dream conversation are the dreamer's image and an unfamiliar figure created to speak for the inner self, and the usual purpose for that conversation is for the "stranger" to provide guiding feedback to the gone-astray conscious self. The inner self is a shepherd.

A pregnant woman dreamed this in a desire section:

I was back home from the hospital holding my new baby boy. An unidentified man was looking at my baby. I said something about newborn babies being ugly. The man replied, "I don't think he's ugly." I looked down at my infant son and saw that he had a perfectly shaped head, blue or green eyes, and was extremely beautiful.

Her words indicate that she consciously tended to think of newborn infants as ugly. Her inner self didn't want her to think that way, and therefore had the other dream speaker express a different view. The plot after that conversation shows that she wanted a beautiful baby, so her conscious attitude didn't eliminate that inner desire.

Another woman dreamed this in her desire section:

I was praying and said, "God, please forgive me." A kindly image of God appeared and said, in an accepting way, "It's all right, I know everything about you."

She consciously was inclined to think she needed spiritual forgiveness, but her inner view--expressed by the religious image--was that she need feel no anxieties about her moral or spiritual worth.

A woman who had recently had surgery dreamed:

I am wearing a red sleeveless dress. I am being helped along through the snow by friends. I protest that I'm just out of the hospital. They reply gently, "That's why we're hurrying you along." We come to a steep terrace resembling Inca steps. It is covered by ice. They want me to go sliding in a crouched position down that ice. I state firmly that I am going to hold on firmly to the railing. I remind them of how much it hurts me when I move.

The conversation which begins in her desire section reveals that her inner self wanted her to be more physically active than she consciously chose to be. She consciously hated the pain movement brought her, but that perspective led to the self-imposed physical inactivity her inner self was trying to overcome.

In this next example, the conversation in a woman's dream shows that at a conscious level she wished to be brave and loyal. Her inner self had a different wish for her, though. Her dream was:

I was not me, but Princess Diana. I was dressed not as I ordinarily would be, but in a style that was more like hers. I was in the palace and I looked to my left and saw Prince Charles. In the dream he looked handsome. An old man, apparently a trusted servant, was showing us through an old, hidden tunnel which led to the outside grounds somewhere behind the palace. He pointed to a huge weeping willow tree and told us to run there and not to come back before it was dark. The tree was so bent over that the leaves swept the ground,

and it was implicit that we were to go there with the express purpose of conceiving an heir.

After dark we ran back through the tunnel, and the same servant told me that I was to run back to the green car parked to the right of the willow tree as there was fighting and it was dangerous. I said that I would not go without my husband, ever. He said that it was my royal duty to do as I was told and that it was very important. So I reluctantly ran to the green car. When I got there I saw that it had a manual shift. I didn't how to use it and the car was jerking forward and backward, but I did manage to advance slowly for a while. There was a lot of shooting and other cars blocked my way, and I was forced to come out. Amid a lot of gunfire, I left the car and felt a terrible pain in my head. Someone said, "The princess has been shot." With that I awoke to a severe migraine.

The woman reported that she worked in a dangerous neighborhood and that recently a man from her office had been assaulted while walking to his car. This real-life incident and the attitudes it aroused in her had led to the conversation in the nondesire section of her dream. Her image's words indicate that she consciously was reluctant to abandon anyone in danger, but the "servant's" words conveyed her inner view that self preservation should be her primary concern at such times. So if she were with someone who was attacked, her inner self would have her run from that violence rather than remain in the vicinity and try to help the victim.

We see that some of her dream is a pleasant fantasy. She would love being a princess in a fairy tale scenario. She desires having a handsome husband and conceiving a child with that man in a romantic setting, such as underneath a weeping willow tree. The image of the servant helps make that initial part of the dream fulfilling to her by giving her the instructions which lead to the opportunity she seeks of becoming pregnant. And perhaps that desirable role by the servant is necessary to make his subsequent guidance about running away more influential to her. In constructing such plots, dreams can be excellent "tacticians."

Some dream conversations are between the dreamer and a person or persons the dreamer knows in everyday life.

A woman dreamed this in a hatred section:

I was in the bed with no clothes on and Don was sitting on the bed. Paula came in and said, "So, what's going on here?" I laughed and then said that I didn't know how it happened. Paula left and Don said, "We must never mention this or do this again." I said that I loved my boyfriend and would not want to do it again.

The dreamer told me that Paula was Don's girl friend, and that the dreamer and Don had recently had an affair. With that background, it becomes apparent the dreamer's conscience was bothering her. Her laughter was opposite emotionality, and helped show her pain and remorse about her sexual activity with Don. Her words as well indicated that she wanted to avoid such infidelity in the future.

So conversations in dreams with familiar people can resemble a soap opera--but in the example that follows a conversation with a familiar person is altogether different in scope and motivation from the previous example, and the related conclusion is that dreams can use conversations in a wide variety of ways to suit their flexible purposes.

A woman who was a jogger and an enthusiast of the space program dreamed this in her dream's love section:

I was in the car with Margie and I was telling her how I wanted to go on the space shuttle and how I wanted to run in place while I was on it. I was really looking forward to doing that. Margie began telling me how much Brad wanted to go on the space shuttle and how lucky I was to be going on it.

The dream was conveying several different loves of the dreamer's: her love for jogging; her love for Margie (since Margie was with her in that section); and her love that Brad (a friend of hers) shared her enthusiasm about the space shuttle. We also can detect within that plot an inner love for the dreamer: the final words from her friend's image telling her she was lucky to be going on the shuttle were designed to make her dream as happy a fantasy as possible. Such an attempt to make a dream happy occurs when the inner self truly loves the dreamer.

We also should look at examples of "unusual" conversations, although none of the conversations in our dreams may ever seem entirely normal.

The first dream that follows is distressing to relate, since it is one of mine and reveals an inner prejudice. But also it shows that dream conversations can include nonverbal responses as well as words.

While living in Oklahoma, I dreamed in the first half of a dream:

I was talking to a beautiful woman. "You're an Okie, just like me," I said. She nodded, looking sad. She seemed to be of partly French ancestry. (I somehow had that knowledge in the dream.)

At the time, I had applied to a Ph.D. psychology program at an Oklahoma university, and was thinking about applying to a similar graduate program at a university in Canada. But Canada was far away, and consciously I felt complacent about staying in Oklahoma. The person I spoke to in my dream felt differently, though. Her partly-French appearance, in conjunction with her sadness about remaining in Oklahoma, was an indication my inner self preferred for me to attend the Canadian university, which was located in a region with a French subculture. Her sad nod about being an Okie implied that attending school in Oklahoma would be acceptable only as a second choice.

In this next example, a conversation occurred in which the dreamer's image didn't participate. A woman dreamed this in her dream's desire section:

A nun who was working in my office said in a sweet, religious voice to the office manager, "What the fuck do you want?" A priest told her to stop. "It's a way of being one of them," she answered. "If you don't stop, you're fired," he said.

This is a complicated and interesting conversation. It suggests two separate conflicts: (1) the dreamer had an urge to use uninhibited language at work, and yet an inner part of her realized it wouldn't be wise to do so; (2) she felt some mixed identities about being a Christian, and a "nun" inside her was more inclined to act freely than an inner "priest." Nor had she reached an inner consensus about which of those roles was more appropriate for her.

That sort of conversation in dreams happens only rarely. The talents in the inner mind usually work together to find one best orientation to even the most complex situations. Such problem solving is an integral part of the value of dreaming.

MISCELLANEOUS COMMUNICATIONS

CREATIVE STYLES OF SPEAKING

Some dreams have figures speak in unusual, idiosyncratic ways. Fortunately, it doesn't take a Sherlock Holmes or a hieroglyphics expert to understand the messages.

I dreamed in the love section of a dream that someone was talking to me.

"Heming(mumble)," that person said.

"Who?" I asked.

"Heming(blur)," was the response.

"Who?" I asked again.

This time the dream character responded with a completely unintelligible word.

What did those mysterious words mean? I had recently written some short stories, and I knew that the mumbling was a means of giving me some writing advice. Here are those words again, followed by their meaning.

"Heming(mumble)": "You need to experiment with your writing style, Dan, and perhaps a suitable style for you would be similar to the way Hemingway wrote. But your ideal style wouldn't be completely identical to his, of course--and therefore the last part of his name is mumbled."

"Heming(blur)": "There's more than one way to imitate Hemingway, and you'll have to experiment to find out which semi-imitation of his style is best for you."

"(The completely unintelligible word)": "You may find that the best style for you doesn't resemble Hemingway's after all. Practice and experimentation will be necessary to find the optimum writing style for you, whatever it might be."

Those writing suggestions appeared in the love section of my dream because my inner self loved my writing efforts.

Incidentally, the meaning of those words wasn't difficult for me to figure out. That was because I was the dreamer and they were on my wavelength. The moral is not to be intimidated by any seemingly weird material in your dreams. You have the capability to understand all of it by being rational and methodical.

What about stuttering or any other speech difficulty when it occurs in a dream? Was it unplanned in the plot, and there only because a dream figure was unable to speak normally? Let's look at the following example before arriving at the answer.

A girl who was taking a psychology class dreamed in the dream's nondesire section that she stuttered as she talked about not being asked out on dates. She had learned in class that stuttering can be caused by inner unhappiness or turmoil, and the dream was using that type of speech to emphasize her feelings of loneliness and rejection (knowing she would understand the stuttering's significance).

So the stuttering was deliberate, and in fact dreams have an immense range of vocal capabilities available to them. Her dream could have shown her speaking as expressively as a talented actress if her inner self had wanted it that way.

We see in this next example how a tone of voice in a dream helped deliver a message. A man had taken part in a contest for amateur comedians. He had been booed, and wasn't sure why. That night he dreamed that a comedian on stage was shouting in a vibrant, enthusiastic voice. Thinking about that afterwards, he realized that during his comedy performance his voice had been uneventful and boring, and his dream was showing him a different, better style of performing.

("It was worth the booing to learn that," he said.)

THE DREAMER VOCALIZES

During some dreams the dreamer will speak out loud. It is no coincidence that those vocalizations tend to awaken the dreamer, since they are a deliberate attempt to draw attention to the related issue, which will be an important one.

For example, a woman who was on the verge of breaking up with her boyfriend and was feeling sad about that spoke these words out loud during the final moments of a dream: "Tumor within five months." Her inner self anticipated her sadness would continue and would be so overwhelming that she would develop cancer as a psychosomatic consequence.

(There was a happy ending. Because of that dream's implication, she and her boyfriend didn't end their relationship, and she didn't develop cancer. Instead, he taught her how to milk cows--but this digresses.)

It isn't just words that are uttered aloud during dreams.

A teenage girl who ate the wrong foods, and too much of them, dreamed in the nondesire section about the pimples on her face and about her plump, unattractive body, and during the hatred section she audibly laughed. That laughter was opposite emotionality, and was designed to alert her to the pain she was experiencing because of the social consequences of her poor eating habits.

Here is a man's account of the ending of a dream of his:

I was dreaming I was out of work and didn't have enough money to pay the bills. I began to cry in the dream and then awakened, still crying. My wife was as surprised as I was.

The dreamer had recently taken a job after having been unemployed for several months, and felt relieved to be earning money again. So the crying in the dream was opposite emotionality. But the crying that continued as he awakened was genuine. It was a means of helping him recover from the stress he'd felt while out of work. His inner self had sensed that the actual crying would do him some good, and therefore had caused it to happen.

Did he consciously feel embarrassed about crying? If so, it didn't matter to his inner self. In general, dreams know what's best for us, and have the power to take over our vocalizing to carry out their constructive purposes.

UNSPOKEN, VISIBLE WORDS

Occasionally, unspoken words appear in the dream plot for the dreamer to see. Those words can be as valuable as any which a dream figure speaks, yet there is a complication to interpreting them. As will be seen in the analysis of the two examples that follow, the unspoken words can't be evaluated solely on their location in the dream. That makes them potentially confusing, and an encompassing analysis is necessary to interpret them correctly.

A man returned to his hometown after an absence and had the option of contacting several women he'd dated in the past. Then he met a woman he felt attracted to, and that night saw in the nondesire section of his dream the unspoken words, "For auld lang syne." On a surface level, those words (which he recognized as being from the sentimental song typically sung on New Year's Eve) seemed to imply he should contact those old friends. The nondesire message, however, was that it would be undesirable to feel any continuing attachment to the prior girlfriends now that he had met that new woman.

In contrast, in this second example unspoken words in the nondesire section of a dream provided a correct perspective despite their nondesire location.

A woman with a seizure disorder had recently been experiencing an increase in seizures. Then she learned from her dentist that her gums were in bad shape and she needed to have several of her teeth pulled. Unsurprisingly, she began feeling depressed about her seemingly deteriorating health. During this same stage of emotional vulnerability, her boyfriend told her he wanted to start dating other women.

One night, after feeling especially sad, she dreamed this in a dream's nondesire section:

**A knight (from a chess set) had lost its bottom half, and its head had
toppled onto the floor. Someone said to it, "You have violated the fire
god." Suddenly, she saw a page from a bible, and on it were the
words, "Christ comforts."**

The knight evidently symbolized both her "lost sexuality" and her
dental problems, since it was missing its bottom half and its head was
shown as being in harmful contact with the floor. The words spoken to that
symbol symbolically attributed her seizures to religious wrath against her.

But that attribution didn't reflect her true inner belief, and was spoken
in that nondesire location only to show it was undesirable to her. Similarly,
the suffering caused by her other problems was undesirable as well, and
the unspoken words in her dream pointed out a spiritual remedy for her
difficulties. The implication of those unspoken words in her nondesire
section was that it would be undesirable for her not to seek religious
solace.

UNSPOKEN WORDS WHICH ARE ALSO MISSPELLED

Having established that unspoken words in the dream can be tricky to
interpret, we now amend that rule. If they are also misspelled, the
interpretation usually will be simple. The misspelling is deliberate, and the
words refer to a hazardous or otherwise flawed real-life situation. The
significance of the misspelling is, in effect, a warning: the dreamer should
either avoid the related situation or, at least, be cautious about it.

For instance, a man who had spent an evening in a smoke-filled room
dreamed that night in the nondesire section the unspoken word, "aer." The
association between that and the smoky room was obvious, and the
meaning was that his inner self wanted him to avoid such polluted air if
possible.

The message in this next example was one of wise pessimism. I had
been planning to take my old car on a long mountain journey. Then I
dreamed in the nondesire section of a license plate which was similar to
the license plate of my car but not identical to it. After awakening, I
realized the purpose of that "misspelled" license plate was to inform me I

probably shouldn't use my car for that trip. My car was not only old but also feeble, and prior to the dream I had been suppressing that fact from my optimistic conscious perspective.

DREAM THOUGHTS

We now come to the last of the special language topics in this chapter, and it turns out to be easy to learn to interpret. When a thought appears in a dream, its value can be determined by its dream pattern location. Any thought appearing in the love or desire section is one the inner self approves of, and any thought in the nondesire or hatred section is considered unwise or inappropriate.

A woman who spoke frequently at meetings dreamed this in the desire section:

A woman was speaking before a group. I realized that she spoke too quickly and didn't look at the audience enough while she presented her information.

Those flaws existed in the dreamer's own speaking style, and it was desirable that she recognize them in that symbol for herself.

A woman dreamed this in the last half of a dream:

I feel that if my daughter is cold I should give her my robe rather than wear it myself. I have mixed feelings inside me. Then I think that I'm happy to do this for her.

The dreamer's inner self didn't want her to sacrifice herself in such ways for her daughter, who was a teenager and able to take care of herself. For that reason, the sentiment about giving the robe to the daughter was undesirable, and the "noble" thought at the end of the dream was one the dreamer would hate.

The thought in this next example might seem justified by its context. Nevertheless, it appeared in the nondesire section of a dream and accordingly was undesirable. A man dreamed in that section:

My girlfriend and I began to get into an argument about which nightclub to go to. I thought she was being selfish and incapable of seeing my point of view.

The dreamer's inner self didn't want him to have that sort of negative thought about his girlfriend even during an argument.

The difference between dream thoughts and dream speech is important to understand. As we have seen, dream speech which occurs in the nondesire or hatred section can convey a correct or normal view about a negative situation. (For example, the unemployed engineer spoke accurately in the nondesire section about his talents.) But any dream thought in the last half of a dream will not be correct or normal in relation to the dreamer's true reality.

With that understanding, this next example becomes comprehensible. A woman dreamed in the nondesire section that some dinner guests failed to compliment her about the food she'd prepared, and then dreamed in the hatred section:

I seemed to say, "I can't stand it." But it was unclear if I had said those words or instead had thought them.

What was the reason for that unusual mixture of speech and thought? It occurred because the woman's inner self had ambivalent feelings about the sentiment her dream image expressed. If being upset because the guests didn't praise her cooking had been fully acceptable to her, the dream would have shown her speaking those words but not thinking them; if being upset in that situation had been totally unacceptable, her dream self would have thought those words but not spoken them. Since she was shown as half-speaking and half-thinking them, the implication is that the temperamental nature they depicted was acceptable to her, but only marginally so.

From such examples, we see how language in dreams is consistent enough to be understandable and yet is sufficiently flexible for the inner self's purposes.

CHAPTER 7

SYMBOLISM

How can we understand symbolism in dreams? Well, some people rely on books which list hundreds or thousands of purported symbols and attempt to explain each by using arbitrary, whimsical definitions. Once, as a joke, I started such a list. "If you dream about Humpty Dumpty falling off a wall," I wrote, "it means he will hit the ground and probably splatter."

The first step to understanding symbolic content in dreams is to use dream pattern analysis. Identify which dream section (or sections) each symbol appears in, and use that information in determining the symbol's emotional significance.

You may have to unravel related complications in the dream plot involving emotionality or speech, but you're able to do that now.

It also helps to know what types of dream messages require symbols. That will be one of the topics we focus on in this chapter.

THE NECESSITY OF USING SYMBOLISM

Why do some dreams use symbols? Often, it is because they must. The dream plot is primarily visual, yet it sometimes must include a message about an abstract concept that isn't easy to show visually. How can such messages be presented? What dreams do in such instances is use a symbol which is visual in nature as a substitute for the complex concept.

Suppose, for example, that the inner self wants to depict in a dream the **amount of love** the dreamer is receiving. How can that amount be indicated? The usual dream solution is to symbolize the love by either of two images: food or money. Both are easy to show in variable quantities, and both are something people perpetually want. That makes them appropriate substitutes to use.

LOVE SYMBOLISM

Some examples of love symbolized as food or money follow.

A girl in a stressful home environment dreamed in the nondesire section of her dream that her stepmother said, "Here's your supper," and handed her a plate with a few bread crumbs on it. That inadequate meal symbolized the small amount of love she was receiving, and that lack of sufficient love was undesirable to her.

A small girl dreamed in the hatred section that her brother spent all her money. The girl basically felt loved--she had a sense of love from her mother and father stored in a mental piggy bank--but the dream shows she was concerned that her brother would receive that love instead, or would otherwise interfere with its coming to her.

The type of food or money can be part of the symbolic message. For example, a man dreamed in the hatred section that he had a big box of popcorn available to him but was too full to eat it. On the previous evening he had intended to go to two separate parties, but after attending the first decided not to go to the second. How did he feel inside about that decision? The dream was expressing his inner regret that he hadn't "eaten" the large amount of "popcorn love" at the second party. (And what is popcorn love? As may have been immediately clear to you, it is love which is enjoyable without being absolutely necessary. A more important or sustaining love likely would be depicted in a dream as a main course: as meat and potatoes, perhaps.)

The contextual use of the symbol within the plot can provide a key part of the symbol's meaning. For example, a woman dreamed in the first half of a dream that she was walking along the beach and suddenly came upon some gold coins half buried in the sand. The dream was conveying her desire to find love (rather than money), and offered some guidance about doing so. The image of the half-buried coins suggested that love was indeed available to her, but she would have to be alert to discover it.

This next dream's love symbolism is relatively apparent in meaning, but nonetheless the dream content contains a mystery. Was the dream a premonition?

A woman dreamed in the first half of a dream of baking a birthday cake for her son and then of having a party for him in the back yard. In that dream's nondesire section she dreamed that the children next door began jumping up and down, and in the hatred section dreamed:

The vibrations from their jumping caused the cake to slide off the table. It broke into a million pieces.

The breaking of the birthday cake in that ending symbolized her hatred of love being totally destroyed. Was that a normal emotion of hatred? If not, why had she dreamed it? What, furthermore, was the link with "vibrations?"

The next morning her son was hit by a car. Had her inner self foreseen something of that nature occurring, and accordingly tried to warn her of it in the dream? It's impossible to answer this with any certainty, and only one thing seems clear: dreaming in a nondesire or hatred section of food ruined or money lost can have grim connotations.

LOSING WHAT ONE WANTS TO KEEP

Some anxieties or fears are common to almost everyone, and consequently show up in predictable ways in people's dreams.

For example, the dream situation of looking for something but not being able to find it typically symbolizes the prospect of losing a related part of one's life. In illustration, a woman having an extramarital affair dreamed in the hatred section that she was looking for her wedding ring, but it was lost. That plot reflected her fear that her affair would jeopardize her marriage.

According to the renowned dream interpreter Sigmund Freud, dreaming that one's teeth fall out can symbolize such themes as castration anxiety or a concern one is losing one's sexual prowess. Of course, we would expect genuine anxiety about such topics to show up only within the last half of a dream, and if one dreams within a love or desire section about one's teeth falling out that symbolism is likely to have a different, positive meaning.

Freud also said that dream symbolism can occur to shield the conscious self from an awareness of "unacceptable" sexual wishes. Is this true? In some instances, yes.

SEXUAL SYMBOLISM

Often, human sexual organs are symbolized, and because those body parts have a characteristic appearance the symbols will be similar or identical from dream to dream. Consider snakes in dream plots, for instance. The following example uses them in a typical way.

A woman dreamed in the love section that a tiny snake crawled out of her wrist while she was with her boyfriend. In the dream's ending, a huge snake came out of her body and she felt very glad that it was out of her. Reader, don't be shocked regarding her sexual feelings. The tiny snake represented her clitoris--the fact that in the dream plot it had come out of her wrist was simply part of the symbolism--and the huge snake represented a penis. The dream pattern messages were that the woman loved having her clitoris aroused by her boyfriend, and she would have hated feeling glad that intercourse was over and her boyfriend's penis had been withdrawn from her body.

Why did that symbolism occur? Sex organs certainly aren't impossible for dreams to show visually (as you may recall from some of your own dreams), so there must have been some other reason for the snake imagery. Probably, the woman's conscious psyche was reluctant to acknowledge those sexual emotions, and that repressive attitude caused the symbolism.

Here is a more complex example. A woman dreamed this:

Polly Sue and I are in a cave with several small children from church. There is a snake in the cave and Polly Sue keeps trying to kill it with a rock. The children and I tell her we are in a sacred space and we don't kill there. Henry, the preacher at church, enters the cave and approaches the snake. It is now a beautiful cobra, with its back and hood inset with brilliant red jewels and sequins. It rises up as Henry speaks a strange language to it, and then it enters a pocket in his pants.

The snake isn't initially a symbol. The dreamer would love being on a church outing to a cave with Polly Sue and the children from church. But snakes sometimes appear in caves, and the desire section plot indicates that if they saw one it would be desirable for Polly Sue to try to kill it. It also would be desirable to the dreamer to lecture her friend about spiritual values, and thereby set a good example for the children. (Poor Polly Sue! She does the dirty work of trying to kill a potentially dangerous snake and receives a lecture as her reward. But we don't know the background for the dreamer's feelings, and Polly Sue may have engaged in some annoying behavior which had upset the dreamer and led to that dream "revenge.")

The snake becomes symbolic in the last half of the dream. In the nondesire section the preacher approaches the cobra, and although the dreamer wouldn't want the preacher to risk his life in this way, there is more meaning involved than that. The cobra becomes beautiful after the preacher approaches it, and then it enters the preacher's pants. The dreamer's inner self doesn't want her to feel that Henry's penis would be beautiful. And what is the meaning of the preacher's "strange language" which causes the snake to rise up? The language which produces that symbolic erection reflects unpreacherlike lust. The dreamer inwardly wouldn't want Henry to express sexual interests or desires while he's with her.

In short, the last half of the dream acknowledges some potential sexual attraction to Henry and recognizes that he might feel the same way toward her, and the nondesire and hatred sections are influencing the dreamer not to respond positively to such sexual inclinations. Evidently, sex with Henry would be a mistake.

Images other than snakes can be used to symbolize sexual anatomy.

A woman dreamed the following in the first half of a dream:

I picked up a man as I was parking my car. He took me into a warehouse where lots of friendly people were meeting. We sat near the counter. He showed me a huge felt banner he had made.

In the context in which the dreamer picks up a man, his huge felt banner undoubtedly is a symbol for his penis, and since that symbol appears in her desire section the implication is that she feels sexual desire for his "huge banner."

A puzzle exists in relation to that dream. I told the dreamer what I thought the banner represented, and she laughed. She then reported that other dreams of hers had shown her engaging in unsymbolized sexuality with male friends. So it would seem that she didn't have a consciously prudish outlook about sex. Why, then, was the symbol used?

Here is my guess. The male figure in her dream was an unfamiliar person, and although she could readily accept her sexual feelings toward friends she wasn't as inclined to recognize a sexual attraction to a stranger. Accordingly, her inner self symbolized the stranger's penis to allow her to remain consciously ignorant about that potentially shocking desire.

THE VARIED USES OF FLYING

Flying in dreams sometimes has a sexual meaning, since it represents a desirable, "nice" form of physical activity which isn't offensive to conscious morals.

A woman dreamed this in the desire section:

I was with two men and saw a group of men ice skating on a distant frozen pond. I said to the men, "I want you to take me there as fast as you can." So they lifted me by the elbows and we flew to the pond.

The assumption is that the dreamer desired sexual relations with cooperative male companions.

A middle-aged man reported that he sometimes dreamed that he wanted to fly. "But then I dream that it's very hard to get off the ground, so I don't even try," he said. It seems probable that the flying symbolized having an erection. Presumably, wanting to "fly" appeared in his desire section and being too discouraged to try appeared in his nondesire section.

But flying won't inevitably symbolize an aspect of sexuality.

A woman wrote to me about her dreams of flying. "I can fly about, and I have such a good time doing so," she said in the letter, "but no one else in my family can, and that's how the dreams usually end." She went on to describe her enjoyable daily life, which included raising a family, being a Girl Scout leader, having a number of friends, and generally being a busy, constructive member of society. So it seems the flying symbolized her positive life adjustment, and the ending reveals she hated the fact that her family lacked what so rewarding to her. She wanted them to experience a similarly excellent lifestyle.

In this next example, flying symbolized neither sexuality nor personal adjustment, and in fact it wasn't a symbol at all. A man on a trip away from home dreamed this in the first half of a dream:

I was up in the air, able to fly, and I flew to my house. I could see lighted windows in the house and knew it was full of friendly people. Then I swooped down to get a better look at my boat that was in the back yard.

The dreamer had been feeling nostalgia for his house and boat, and the flying was a convenient way for his dream image to visit them.

THE USE OF A PROP

The flying in that dream could be considered a prop which helped to advance the plot. Here is another instance in which a dream used a prop. Shortly after the death of a friend, a man dreamed this:

There was a knock at the door and there stood Howard (the dead friend). He was dressed in a new gray suit and was wearing a hat. In

my dream I thought this odd, because I had never seen him wear a hat. My whole family and I were overjoyed to see him. We invited him in and I remember saying how good it was to see him. He responded that it was sure good to see us, too. We talked for a while, although I can't remember anything specific that we talked about. Then he said that he had to go because he couldn't stay long. We followed him out onto the porch and waved goodbye to him, and then went back inside and started crying because we knew we'd never see him again. While we were crying, a gentle tap came at the door. I opened it and Howard said, "Say, I forgot my hat."

By returning for his hat, the image of Howard interrupted and contradicted the dreamer's grief. The underlying message was that the dreamer's inner self hated for him to mourn his dead friend too much, since that wouldn't have been in the spirit of their friendship.

Examples such as that remind us that dreams can be kind to the conscious self.

PEOPLE AS SYMBOLS

The creative use of people's images is another tool which dreams can use to present symbolic messages.

A man reported this about the beginning of a dream of his:

Robert (a talented guitarist) was using my guitar. He was playing in the key of F, which I usually avoid because of its difficulty.

Robert was a symbol of the dreamer as he could become. The dreamer's inner self would love it if he could play the guitar as Robert did, including in the key of F.

A woman dreamed this in the desire section:

I was in a session with my psychoanalyst. A strange woman wandered through the office and sat in another room. I went to see about her.

She said she needed food. I told my therapist, and he went to take care of her.

The other woman was speaking for the dreamer's inner self, and the request for food was a symbolic way of asking for love. Yet although the woman needed love from her therapist she apparently had difficulty in acknowledging that consciously, since a stranger in her dream had to ask for the love.

While I was working in a psychology position, I needed to have my teeth checked, but I was procrastinating about scheduling the visit to the dentist. Then I dreamed in the hatred section that my supervisor was drilling on my teeth. That supervisor was efficient at pointing out my mistakes, which I apparently committed in great quantities while working there, so the dream was using his image as a dentist to show me that I was making a mistake in postponing the dental exam. Nor was that the only reason for his appearance in my dream. I didn't enjoy seeing him in the dream plot, and of course my inner self knew that. The implied communication to me was, "You'll see this sort of unpleasantness in your dreams if you neglect your health."

Such dream experiences are part of the spectrum of dreaming. The inner self sometimes feels disappointed or unhappy with the conscious self, and may choose to produce unpleasant dreams as a consequence. Yet the inner self has the best interests of the conscious dreamer at heart, and is always working to provide benevolent messages as well as adaptive ones in dreams. You often may find, in fact, that your dreams will be forgiving and supportive when you wouldn't have expected them to be so.

One such example of a dream which shows that forgiveness and support follows.

I had decided to play in a chess tournament in New York, even though I would be staying at an expensive hotel, I had little chance to win a prize because of the talented competition, and there were competing attractions in my home town during the period of the tournament. I had several dreams, furthermore, which tried to dissuade me from going. A stern figure in one of them told me I would have to play virtually mistake-free chess. Another dream showed me other, better ways to spend my money than on the trip. Nevertheless, I traveled to the tournament, and on the night before the first round I dreamed this in the desire section:

A man was speaking to a boy next to me. "Going to beat them, Dan?" that figure asked the boy. The speaker then growled in a playful voice: "Grrr, grrr."

I saw that my inner self didn't have a grudge against me because I'd gone to the tournament. The speaker in the dream wanted me to do well in the tournament and he also wanted me to enjoy it. His words were to the image of a boy rather than to me because I consciously wasn't as much on his wavelengths as the boy was. My inner self had decided that the tournament was a time for the youthful abdication of adult roles, and the growls were playfully designed to stimulate my fighting spirit.

ANIMAL SYMBOLISM

An animal which appears in a dream plot can be part of a symbolic message. This seems to be common knowledge in relation to sexual themes. Yet sexuality won't be the only context in which an animal in a dream can be symbolic.

A woman who was experiencing problems in freeing herself from her mother's influence dreamed this in the first half of a dream:

I am in the pasture where I used to play as a child. I am a panther-- shiny black, strong, and capable.

The image of the panther reflected the beautiful capabilities the dreamer sensed in herself. But the dream also was about the desirable freedom she sought from her mother, who years ago hadn't wanted her to be in that pasture alone. Being a panther would end all her mother's concerns for her safety, and consequently the dreamer could have a clear conscience to do as she wished.

Animal symbolism can be religious in nature. For example, a woman dreamed the following not long after her atheist brother had died in an accident:

I caught a large fish. I must have used my hands and not a pole, because I had it in an aquarium and decided to take it to my brother as a gift for his aquarium. So I started out walking to his house carrying the fish, but the longer I walked the farther away his house became. The fish began gasping to be returned to the water, so for fear it would die I hurried back to my own aquarium and placed the fish in it. The fish floated on its side for a few seconds and then returned to normal. I felt awful that I was unable to complete my journey.

The woman was a devout Christian, and since a fish is a well-known symbol of Christian faith the dream appears to be revealing the woman's wish to have given her brother Christianity.

The dream contains other symbolism as well, and knowledge of the dream pattern helps us understand it. Arriving at her brother's house presumably symbolized dying, since it was desirable to the dreamer to become farther away from that house rather than closer to it. The uncompleted journey in the hatred section symbolized the realization that it was too late to be helpful to her brother. Note that the focus of the hatred was on feeling awful rather than on not completing the journey. Her inner self didn't want her to experience the perpetual pain involved with hating a situation she never would be able to change.

What does the nondesire plot about the fish gasping for breath and then recovering its health mean? The answer is not obvious and the dreamer was not available for questioning, so a guess becomes necessary. The recovery occurred in the dreamer's aquarium, and so her inner self may have been making a metaphorical statement about the undesirability of not taking risks in giving gifts to others. In that context, a healthy fish in her own aquarium would be less desirable than an unhealthy fish in someone else's. Overall, the dreamer innately wanted to be generous with others.

As noted, some animal symbolism will present a sexual message.

A woman who liked to ride horses dreamed the following in the desire and nondesire sections:

I was riding on the back of a magnificent stallion. It was running faster than seemed possible. Then an incredible thing happened: the horse instantaneously stopped and then shot up like a rocket. Next, there was a transformation, and I was catapulted into the sky and the horse was gone, and instead I was suspended within a two-dimensional, spinning rectangle. Jack, my boyfriend at the time, was there and I wanted to touch him, but the centrifugal force prevented this.

The dreamer reported that Jack had never wanted her to get physically affectionate with him. The logical conclusion is that the stallion ascending "like a rocket" symbolized sexual activity with a more willing boyfriend.

In the nondesire plot, the centrifugal force evidently symbolized the restraints her boyfriend had imposed upon their physical relationship, since that force prevented her from touching him. Another implication is that the lack of touching caused her to feel two-dimensional when with him, rather than being fully herself.

"PHILOSOPHY" IN DREAMS

Dream symbols can convey philosophical or metaphorical meanings. Such symbols usually won't depict the academic concepts one finds in philosophy classes, however. The inner self tends to be more down to earth than that.

A pregnant woman due to go into labor dreamed in a love section that she crossed a river without difficulty. The remainder of that dream was about her new child, so the beginning clearly was symbolic for giving birth. The image of crossing a river was soothing to her, and could help her think calmly about the birth that was soon to occur.

A college student had a job as a gatekeeper at a landfill outside of town. The job wasn't a demanding one, and allowed him to study and do other homework there. One night he dreamed in the desire section that he was working at that job, but the surrounding area had become a beautiful nature park: the mud and weeds and cattle and cattle manure had been transformed into lush vegetation and exotic animals. The metaphorical message was that his job was a beautiful one.

A man dreamed the following:

I could see my baby, but as a spinal column rather than as an entire baby. I thought the baby was too tall, and decided to cut off some of his spinal column. The knife wouldn't cut through the spinal column very well. Then the baby couldn't move, and the doctor told me it was because the baby's spinal column had been injured.

"What does the dream mean?" the dreamer asked me.

I recognized that the spinal column was symbolic, but of what? "Did anything happen the previous evening that might be related to the dream?" I asked the man.

"I had to discipline my son for making too much noise."

That made the meaning clear. The spinal column was a metaphorical symbol for the concept of discipline. The dreamer loved viewing his child as requiring discipline. It was desirable to him to discipline his son. It would be undesirable if the discipline didn't work well, and he would hate it if his son came to harm because of being over-disciplined.

That symbolism served an informative purpose. The dreamer was an electronics technician in real life, and the dream was revealing that his technical orientation at that job affected his parenting. The image of him adjusting the length of his baby's spinal column indicated that he viewed disciplining his child as being similar to fixing a machine that was malfunctioning. Did his inner self like that view? Undoubtedly not, and the symbolism was designed to alert him to it. Becoming aware of such thinking is the first requirement for changing it.

SYMBOLIC SPEECH

As shown in the previous chapter, speech in dreams can have a symbolic meaning. This next example contains such speech in the midst of other symbolic content. A woman dreamed this:

I am at a church camp. There is a high bluff. I am in the front seat of a car and Kathy, a teen member of the church, is in the back. Julie, Kathy's sister, had been pushing from the rear of the car toward the bluff but then she goes to the front of the car and pushes. I am trying everything I can to stop the car. The brakes will not stop us; the gears will not stop us. I am doing everything I know to do but we are still headed toward the bluff. I say to Kathy, "Doesn't she understand that when I go off the bluff it will hurt her as much as me?"

The dreamer was an official for a church that had an outdoor camp near a high bluff. The mother of Kathy and Julie had been trying to get the dreamer fired from her church job. Kathy liked the dreamer, though, and didn't want to see her fired. Julie initially had opposed the dreamer but had finally begun liking her also.

That information helps in understanding the dream. The dreamer loved being at the church camp. The car moving toward the bluff symbolized the danger the dreamer would lose her job, and so Kathy's presence in the car with her symbolized Kathy's support for her. That support was desirable, of course, as was Julie's attempt to push from the front of the car rather than from the rear as she previously had been doing. The nondesire section showed the dreamer's anxiety that she wouldn't be able to prevent the loss of her job. Her speech in the dream ending was stating her awareness that if she were fired, the girls' mother (referred to as "she") also would be hurt due to the pain her daughters would feel. The mother didn't understand that, and the dreamer hated her lack of understanding.

Why did the symbolism occur? Was it to continue the pleasant plot about being in the vicinity of the church camp? But dreaming about a car moving toward a bluff certainly isn't pleasant, and in fact the perilous driving was reflecting a separate concern of the dreamer's that she would be unable to stop her car if it actually were moving downward toward a bluff. So there were two different sets of messages in the plot, and in order to present both the dream had to use symbolism. Only the more complicated theme was symbolized, however. Dreams don't use symbols when they don't have a good reason to do so, and the simpler concern about the car going out of control was shown directly in the plot.

AN ARTIST'S DREAM

Why else do dreams use symbolism besides the reasons we have already examined? The man who had this next dream was an artist, and some of the symbolism in it may have occurred to exercise his artistic capabilities. He dreamed:

My wife and I were at our daughter's house. In the den, Eileen, my daughter, has one of those new-fangled lamps--nothing more than a white globe with a bulb in it. A transformation had taken place in the lamp. Instead of the globe, there was the lamp base. Over it had been stretched a transparent balloon which was filled with water. On closer inspection I expected to see a fish in the water, but instead there was a parrot which was moving but making no perceptible sounds. When I expressed concern over what would happen if the balloon broke (noting that fish quickly die when removed from water), Eileen laughed gaily. At exactly this moment the balloon assumed the shape of an upside-down beet, and became beautifully green in color. While before its surface had been dull, it now was as glistening as glass. Moreover, the "beet" began widening steadily in girth and flattening at the bottom and top. It was like a huge doughnut without the hole. I was standing in front of it when it suddenly burst with a noise resembling escaping steam. In the background, an unidentified man was taking all of this in. He was a visitor, interested in what was going on but unknown to us. When the "beet" or balloon broke, my wife said, "You had a microphone right there beside the globe. What did he say?" By "he," she did not mean the unknown visitor, but an announcer who had not even been in the dream previously. I rushed

over, picked up the microphone, and shouted into it, "Mein gott, the Hindenburg is on fire." Everyone laughed except the unknown visitor, who politely smiled.

The dreamer sent me this dream in a letter, and his comments regarding the dream content were only these: his daughter owned a lamp similar to the one which had undergone a transformation in his dream; she had a parrot who sometimes made a lot of noise; and she also had an aquarium which looked pretty but which required a lot of work.

With just that minimal information, is it possible to make any sense of the dream? The answer is yes, and in fact we can understand quite a bit of it. The basic processes of dream interpretation we've learned in this book explain much.

The dream begins with the dreamer and his wife visiting their daughter. The dreamer loves such visits. As the love section continues, the modernistic lamp undergoes a transformation. From this we conclude that he doesn't like the lamp as it is, since he would love for it to change. The lamp begins to resemble an aquarium, but one which contains a quiet parrot rather than fish, and it seems the dreamer likes the appearance of his daughter's aquarium but isn't as fond of the fish in it, and instead he prefers the company of the parrot--when it's not being too noisy. Next, the dreamer states a concern that the fish might die and his daughter responds with opposite-emotionality laughter. Presumably, she shares that concern as well. Does the daughter find it difficult to keep the ecological conditions inside the aquarium safe for the fish, and is that the source for their anxiety? In any case, the dreamer wants his daughter to feel merriment about the aquarium, since that is the dream pattern message regarding her laughter in his desire section. The additional changes the lamp undergoes are artistic in nature, and reflect either desirable or undesirable changes to him. (It's unclear where his desire section ends and his nondesire section begins, and only the dreamer could pinpoint this transition.) The lamp, in a symbolized form, breaks in the nondesire section, and therefore that would be undesirable to him, but perhaps only because of the sadness his daughter would feel. The announcer provides a microphone the dreamer can speak into; the implication is that he would like to express inner thoughts about the lamp which he has been concealing. His words about the destruction of the Hindenburg reveal excitement and pain: the excitement is shown in the words themselves, and the pain is implied by their location in his hatred section. That statement of his, which superficially seems to be irrelevant to the dream plot, implies that in contrast to the Hindenburg's destruction the breaking of the lamp would be a trivial thing. The unknown visitor is a symbol for the dreamer, and so that visitor's polite, opposite-emotionality smile reveals what the dreamer would feel if the lamp actually broke: a mild, superficial pain. We conclude from this dream that the lamp had offended his artistic sensibilities.

Whether you're an artist or not, or--more to the point--whether your dreams are even more complicated than this one, any symbolism in them needn't prove confusing or mysterious. Initially, use dream pattern analysis. Analyze any complications present involving emotionality or speech. Remember what you've now learned about why dreams use symbols.

Be rational and methodical in such ways, and you'll find the symbolism in your dreams can become transparently clear in meaning.

CHAPTER 8

NIGHTMARES

What causes nightmares? Inescapable anxiety or fear certainly can be one source, yet perhaps the most typical reason is that the dreamer isn't adapting as well to reality as he or she should, and the inner self becomes upset about that and produces a nightmare as deliberate punishment. This may seem surprising, since we've seen many examples of the benevolence dreams can display. Yet the inner self has not abandoned its constructive nature during even the worst of those planned nightmares. Invariably, part of such a dream (although not necessarily the nightmarish content itself) will indicate what the dreamer's maladaptive behavior is. So the inner hope is that the dreamer will be alerted by the nightmare, think about the dream, identify the incorrect adaptation, and realize the need to change.

DELIBERATE NIGHTMARES

A man dreamed the following in the last half of a dream:

I wasn't trying to improve the poor relationship I had with my girlfriend. Then I was attacked by a gang of criminals. They were hitting me and the only way I could escape was by awakening. But I couldn't awaken and they continued to hit me.

The dreamer admitted that he and his girlfriend had been drifting apart at that time, but their problems were solvable. So he'd been neglectful about that important aspect of his life, and the nightmare was the result.

A woman dreamed of being at the dentist's office, and reported this about the dream ending:

The dentist picked up one of the dental instruments and began scraping at my teeth and gums in an unpleasant way. I decided I wanted to go and then I could see an ugly old woman sitting there. She said something to the dentist such as, "She'll be back." It was very sinister and foreboding.

The dreamer hadn't been taking good care of her teeth, and that nightmare was the consequence. The old woman's words were alerting the dreamer about a possible dental reality awaiting her, and the frightful nature of the plot was a deliberate means of motivating her to avoid that reality.

Even schoolchildren can upset the person within and suffer nightmares due to inner retribution. A girl taking a trigonometry class dreamed this in the last half of a dream:

A disciplinarian chased me into a giant math book. I was trapped inside that book. Sines and cosines were chasing me.

The girl said she had that dream at a time when she hadn't opened her math book for over two weeks. Her inner self was responding with that plot.

So nightmares can occur when the unconscious mind has run out of patience with the conscious self. And sometimes the nightmares are in response to the dreamer's flawed conscious thoughts, as these next two examples indicate.

A depressed woman who had begun viewing dying as an easy way of escaping from her troubles dreamed in the nondesire section of being in a stressful car accident, and in the hatred section dreamed this:

I felt pinned and was having trouble breathing. Then I thought it was okay to die. I just had to accept it.

One purpose of the dream was to cause her to equate having a complacent attitude about dying with being in a frightening situation such as a car crash. Her inner self hated her conscious mindset that death was an acceptable outcome, and was trying to influence her by the dream's stressful content to avoid such thinking in the future.

A man had been worrying about the various dangers in the world, and that in turn led him to restrict the places he took his son so that the two of them would remain "safe." One night he had a nightmare. That dream didn't begin badly: in its first half he took his son to the fair and they rode a Ferris wheel there. In the nondesire section, the Ferris wheel pitched them into the sea. In the hatred section, he dreamed this:

I started to swim up through the water, carrying my son in my arms, but then I could sense the iron girders of the broken Ferris wheel forming a barrier above me. I realized I was going to die.

That frightening plot wasn't trying to warn him about ferris wheels and drowning. Its purpose instead was to drive home the message that he inwardly hated gloomy thinking.

THE BEARER OF BAD TIDINGS

Unpleasant dreams won't always be that way because the dreamer has done something wrong. On some occasions, the inner self simply has to present an unhappy message about reality. For example, a woman who worked at a day-care center dreamed in the nondesire section of her dream that a child was deformed, but only she could see that. Afterwards, she wondered why she'd dreamed that scene. "It gives me shivers to think about it," she told me. "Is it going to come true?"

In a sense, it already had. Some of the children at the day-care center had emotional and developmental problems which were obvious to the dreamer (and at an inner level she felt those problems were as noticeable as if they were physical deformities). Other staff seemed to overlook them, however, and the dreamer couldn't help the children overcome their problems all by herself. That combination of undesirable elements resulted in the dream plot which was virtually a nightmare.

The nightmare which follows would rank high on anyone's scariness scale, and it apparently didn't occur because of any flaw in the dreamer. A man who took part in bicycle races dreamed this in the hatred section:

I was led into a cell. Some of the bicyclists I compete against were imprisoned there, in chains. There was a pile of human bones in the middle of the cell, and the implication was that the bicyclists had been forced to practice cannibalism in order to survive. I would be a prisoner there, also.

What was the reason for the nightmare's intensity? The man reported that there formerly had been close friendships among the competing bicyclists. Recently, though, they had been experiencing conflicts about racing conditions and prizes, and their warm feelings seemed to be disappearing. That dream ending was showing the man's considerable concern that the bicyclists, against their will, had already "eaten" much of the love that existed within the group, and that he too might have to become just as "cannibalistic." So the underlying theme was about a truly frightening topic: love that is being lost.

THE SHOCKING TRUTH

Some nightmares occur because of an inner feeling that is appalling to the conscious self.

A woman was baby-sitting in her home for her grandson. He pulled the cat's tail, broke her best vase, and misbehaved in other ways as well. That night she had a dream which became a nightmare. She saw her grandson in the dream ending. He wasn't performing any hateful action in the dream, but nevertheless she moaned twice, audibly, as she saw him. It was as if she had seen something horrible.

What was disturbing to her? The logical assumption is that after she saw his image in her hatred section she immediately realized, even while asleep, that she hated him. She didn't want to feel that way and yet she did, and that ungrandmotherly emotion horrified her.

Dreams such as that provide evidence that the conscious mind doesn't totally stop functioning after one falls asleep: it was the dreamer's conscious self who was reacting with moans. And here is another illustration of a dismayed conscious response to a dream in progress. A woman who regularly attended church reported this about a dream:

I was looking at designs of material in a fancy department store. A saleslady held up a beautiful print. There was a woman's face in the print and suddenly her lips began to move. "Jesus is coming," she said. I felt Jesus was coming to me. I began gasping in shock, and my husband awakened me.

She hated the Christian sentiment in the dream ending, and it shocked her to realize that.

Our intuitive understanding of dreams vanishes as we awaken. The conscious dream interpreter can't rely on instincts or intuitions, and instead must turn to rational analysis.

AN IMPROBABLE LOCATION FOR NIGHTMARES

Ordinarily, nightmares are confined to the nondesire or hatred sections of dreams; the love and desire sections usually will contain happy plots. So even if a dream seems nightmarish in its first half (to anyone besides the dreamer), it probably won't have been experienced that way.

Here is an exciting dream a boy had:

I was kidnapped by pirates and taken to Central Park. An animal similar to Big Bird led me into a haunted castle. It took me down into a pit and then it flew back up. I was left there, alone.

The first half wasn't disturbing to him: in his imagination he wanted to experience the adventure of being kidnapped by pirates and being taken to a haunted castle. Being left alone, in contrast, would be something he'd hate.

When the dreamer's inner self is seeking constructive revenge, though, dream material in the first half might genuinely be unpleasant. For example, at a time when a woman was obsessed with dental hygiene and brushed her teeth a dozen or more times a day, she dreamed the following in her desire section:

Some friends and I were window-shopping at the mall. But there was a three-headed person following us around the whole time. The middle head was mad because his teeth never got brushed.

Her tooth-brushing obsession was one she was capable of overcoming, and because she hadn't yet done so her dream presented that desirably-revengeful plot in which a bizarre person spoiled her fun. (It was also desirable, at an inner level, to imagine someone whose teeth were being neglected. The dream plot was allowing the dreamer's inner self to "escape" from a tedious reality in that way.)

A TYPICAL THEME IN NIGHTMARES

In deliberate nightmares one often is unable to move quickly while trying to escape from enemies or danger. Here is an example of that scenario. A man dreamed:

I'm walking in the country with Rex, my dog. He starts barking. He goes somewhere, and then comes back, excited. I follow him as he runs ahead. Then I see him lying on the ground, bleeding. There is a UFO nearby, and they obviously have hurt him. I pick Rex up and we go back to my house. The UFO follows. I can only move in slow motion, and the aliens are catching up. Then I get to my house and Rex revives, and he fights the aliens while I hide inside the house.

This obviously was a nightmare designed to punish the dreamer: the theme involving enemy aliens from outer space wasn't something he realistically would fear, and the involuntary nature of his slow-motion movements was a deliberate means of increasing the tension he experienced. So what had he done wrong to deserve that plot? The hatred message was that he shouldn't hide while his dog was fighting a mutual enemy of theirs, and perhaps his "crime" had involved something of that nature, such as not coming to the dog's rescue when another dog was acting in a threatening manner.

Not all dreams about an inability to move will be deliberate punishment, however. For instance, a woman in love with a married man dreamed in the hatred section that she was unable to touch him. Because she subsequently would hate that, her dream evidently was motivating her to have an affair with him despite the adultery involved. From her conscious point of view, her inner self may have been displaying questionable morals, yet her inner self had its own standards. Nor would she have been punished with nightmares if she did have that affair. In fact, she might have continued to have stressful dreams if she didn't initiate some affectionate physical contact with him.

THE OTHER SIDE OF NIGHTMARES

None of us consciously chooses to have nightmares, but they are designed to help us change to a more adaptive lifestyle. Anyone doing that adapting probably then will begin having much happier dreams. The inner self can reward as well as punish.

CHAPTER 9

QUESTIONS AND ANSWERS ABOUT DREAMS

Q. Why is it important to pay attention to dreams?

They bring messages from a part of the mind that keeps a close watch on both the conscious self and the outside world. That watchfulness pays its dividends in the deep, rich understanding dreams display. So the correct interpretation of dream messages can help the dreamer adapt successfully to life's problems and opportunities.

Q. Is dream interpretation a difficult procedure?

It shouldn't be. The messages are right there waiting to be seen. Simply use dream pattern analysis as you've learned to do in this book, and, as necessary, apply the theories about dream complications which have been presented in recent chapters. You will become aware of what your inner emotions are, and will be able to use that awareness in all sorts of valuable ways.

Here is an example of how that input from the unconscious can lead to a significant change in lifestyle. A woman was busy with her business career. One night she dreamed in a desire section that she was nursing a baby, and in her hatred section of that dream saw that the baby was missing because of something she'd forgotten. Because of her preoccupation with her career, she'd "forgotten" to have the baby she inwardly desired. At a conscious level, though, it wasn't mere forgetting, since she hadn't realized she wanted a child. Her face showed great interest as I explained her dream to her.

Q. When interpreting other people's dreams for them, should the various sexual desires, death wishes, and other potentially shocking messages present in some of that dream content be freely mentioned?

My experience has been that if those messages aren't symbolized, their interpretation won't shock the dreamer. If symbolism is present, though, it might be indicating that the dreamer's conscious self isn't fully ready to understand the inner meaning.

A woman asked me to analyze a dream that included a plot in the desire section in which she and her male cousin looked wordlessly at each other. I tried to be tactful. "Desire sections often have messages involving sex. Is it possible you might have sexual feelings for that cousin of yours? If so, those feelings could easily be triggered when the two of you exchange glances. But there might be some other explanation of why that eye contact with him would be desirable to you."

She looked amused. "It's quite possible I could have sexual feelings for him," she said. "We had a torrid love affair when we were both 17."

Another woman told me a dream that began as follows: "It was night. My husband had just driven away."

She looked sensitive and moody. I was silent for a few seconds, trying to find the best words before interpreting that love section for her. "We all need time to ourselves, and your dream is indicating that you love having that free time when your husband drives away at night. Presumably, you do constructive or relaxing things then."

She laughed heartily.

As we soon shall see, this next dream contains sexual symbolism in its nondesire section. Initially, a woman dreamed in the love section:

I remember seeing Jack and his wife, Debbie. It was as if I were seeing Debbie through a camera because her image started zooming in closer. The closer she got, the uglier she became. I thought, "Jack is married to her?"

In the dream's desire section, she dreamed about going on a picnic with two female friends. Then, in the nondesire section, she dreamed this:

We drifted outside to a blanket and Janet was lying there with Anne and they didn't have their clothes on. I didn't have mine on either and Janet and I lay next to each other on the blanket. We were all getting very sexual and I was feeling very hot. I looked at Janet's body and she had a penis. We were all touching each other and feeling very sensual.

The love plot implies that the dreamer was attracted to Jack, since she would have loved for his wife to be ugly, or instead have personality flaws which the ugliness may have been a symbol for. The accompanying hope was that a wife with flaws would cause Jack's marriage to be unstable.

Nevertheless, Jack **was** married, and in the dreamer's frustration she was potentially willing to turn to women lovers. The scene on the blanket with Janet depicts that tendency of hers. But why was Janet shown as having a penis? Perhaps it was because the dreamer, even though she consciously could become attracted to women, also preferred at a conscious level to see her dream image making love with a "man" than with her female friend. (The conscious self can be complicated and contradictory in that way.) In any case, it is clear that the lesbian lovemaking was undesirable to her inner self, since that sexual scene appeared in her nondesire section. So in addition to containing symbolism regarding a sensitive topic, the dream was indicating a conflict between her conscious inclination to make love with women and her inner wish not to.

The dreamer told me that dream as an example of the "weird" dreams she sometimes had. "I told Janet afterwards I dreamed she had a penis. She thought it was hysterical," she said.

"That plot seems to contain some sexual implications. Would you like me to try to explain them to you?" I asked her.

She blushed. "No," she said. "I'd rather not have it analyzed to death."

Q. Sometimes we're aware in our dreams that we're dreaming. Do those plots follow the same emotional sequence as other dreams?

Yes, so those lucid dreams (as they are called) are analyzed in the usual way. Two examples follow.

A woman dreamed this in the last half of a dream:

Suddenly I realized I was dreaming. Since it was a dream I could do whatever I wanted. So I began doing a strip-tease dance until I was naked from the waist up. Then I said to the men present, "Now which of you sorry sons of bitches wants to marry this lovely creature?"

The strip-tease in the nondesire section was not undesirable to the dreamer. What was undesirable was the awareness that she was dreaming, and therefore her strip-tease wasn't happening outside of her dream. In other words, she wanted to act in that uninhibited way in real life but felt she couldn't.

Her words in the hatred section reveal a resentment toward men, and also show that she wanted to get married in spite of that resentment. We see that her dream plot, despite her awareness in it that she was dreaming, was about basic, down-to-earth feelings.

A man on a business trip dreamed in a love section that he was back at home. In the hatred section he realized he was dreaming, and wasn't at home after all. The purpose of that lucid dreaming was simply to reveal how he felt about being away from home.

You may find books that tell you lucid dreams can have all sorts of insights and adventures in them. That is correct, but dreams which don't include that awareness of dreaming can possess those same qualities.

Q. What about the dreams of mentally ill people? Wouldn't at least some of those dreams deviate from the regular pattern in order to be unusual or bizarre?

The dreams of mentally ill people contain the same emotional pattern as those of normal people.

For example, a woman in a mental institution dreamed in a dream ending that she was wrapped in concrete, and no one could touch her. The dream symbolically was showing her isolation from others, and was revealing her hatred of that isolation. So it was providing valuable information, and the lesson is that dreams don't stop functioning well when the dreamers are mentally ill. In fact, their messages at such times could play a key role in helping the dreamer recover.

Q. Do dreams that reveal the spiritual world have an emotional pattern in their plots?

By way of answer, let's look at the following beautiful dream, which seems to contain an appearance by a dead person's spirit. A woman dreamed this, several months after her son had died in an accident:

I was standing above a road by a building trying to mentally urge a boy on the road to go on. A person in white to the side said the boy would not go on until he talked with me. So I went around a fence and the boy walked back to me. We both looked across to the ruined building across the fence and road. It was like a ruined Greek temple. The boy said, "Pay attention to the light. It transforms things and makes them beautiful." Then he turned and walked off down the road. Only when he was out of reach did I recognize him as my son.

Had her inner self contacted (or been contacted by) the spiritual world, and was her son's spirit actually talking to her? Regardless, her dream can be interpreted by dream pattern analysis. She altruistically wanted her son to advance to his spiritual destiny, and he wanted to speak with her first because of his love for her. The "ruined Greek temple" was a desirable symbol for the destruction of her son's life. His words in the nondesire section offered a way for her to get over her death; the implicit message is that her adjustment at the time of the dream was undesirable. The ending indicates that she'd hate not having a chance to display intimacy or affection for her son because of not recognizing him in his spiritual form.

The great consistency in dreams is that if there's no disruption by an unexpected environmental influence such as a noise, every dream begins with a depiction of what the dreamer loves, continues with what is desirable, proceeds to what is undesirable, and ends with what is hated. This pattern is present in dream content regardless of whether the dream is a lucid one, or has been dreamed by a mentally ill person, or apparently contains telepathy, or has fairy-godmother figures in it, or features a creative use of language, or otherwise seems exotic or unusual.

Sigmund Freud--the most renowned dream interpreter in history-- didn't state that dreams contain a love-desire-nondesire-hatred pattern. Neither did anyone else in the past.

But what do you think now about whether dreams follow that pattern or not?

Q. According to Freud, anyone trying to understand a dream should use "free association" in relation to it: should say whatever spontaneously comes to mind regarding it as a means of understanding its messages. Does that procedure have any value to it?

Producing random chains of associations to dream material ordinarily won't help much. The associations quickly create a web of diverting material which doesn't explain the dream.

Yet free association can be a useful tool at times, if it's combined with dream pattern analysis. An example follows. A man dreamed at the end of a dream of receiving car registration papers and accompanying monthly bills to pay. Subsequently, he asked me what it meant. I explained the dream pattern to him but he still couldn't figure out that part of his dream. He didn't know why he would feel hatred for any such bills, since his car was already paid for. We decided he should try the free association technique in relation to that dream material. Almost immediately, the associations reminded him that his girlfriend had purchased a used car, and he'd agreed to help her make the payments on it. He realized that he would hate doing so.

That free association process was helpful because he was already on the right track: he was looking for associations that would uncover a feeling of hatred. But without a preliminary understanding provided by dream pattern analysis, free associations to dream material are much less likely to lead to the correct interpretations.

Q. I told a psychoanalyst I had dreamed about the death of someone who was alive, and he said I had a death wish toward that person. Is that true?

Not necessarily. In fact, such a statement stands an approximately fifty percent chance of being untrue. If you dreamed about the person's death somewhere within the first half of your dream, then the chances are high you felt a genuine death wish toward him or her. But if you dreamed about the death within the last half of your dream it's highly probable you instead wanted that person to continue living.

Let's look at some dreams in which the death of a living person is featured.

A woman dreamed this:

My married cousin living in South Africa was killed along with her husband in some type of bombing. My aunt and uncle were there trying to clean up the mess and arrange to have my cousin's three small children brought back to the United States. There was some sort of problem with the government there and they were not able to bring the children home.

The deaths of the dreamer's cousin and her husband occurred in the love section, so the dreamer evidently wished for their deaths. The remainder of the dream indicates why she had that wish. It would be desirable if her aunt and uncle tried to bring the children back; undesirable if there were governmental red tape that interfered with that goal; and the dreamer would hate it if the children could not be brought home. It becomes clear the dreamer had hostile feelings toward the children's parents for raising them in a foreign country.

Another woman dreamed this:

I am on the expressway close to downtown Chicago. At the corner of State and Congress there is some construction going on. The previous building had been razed and cleared away, leaving a very deep hole. It is a sunny and beautiful day. As I peer over the construction fence to

see what is going on, I realize that I see my father lying face down, dead. The other workers carry on, not noticing.

This time the death was in the nondesire section, so it would be undesirable to the dreamer if her father were to die. One wonders what special reason caused her to dream this. Wouldn't it be normal for her to feel his death would be undesirable (or something to be hated)? Why did her dream present such an "obvious" message?

The dreamer said that following a turbulent adolescence, she had been able to establish close friendships with all of her family except her father. She sometimes regretted not having a better relationship with him. That explains the dream's purpose. It was reminding her that his death would be undesirable to her, and in that way was trying to motivate her to establish that closer relationship.

A woman reported she had dreamed as a girl of 11:

It was night and there was a full moon. I was walking in the woods. I came upon some garbage cans. Then I saw my brother's body lying dismembered in one of those garbage cans.

The woman said that a month later her brother was killed in a knife fight. Naturally, she wondered if her inner self had been aware of that in advance. "When I had that dream, did I know deep down inside that my brother would die?" she asked me.

It was a question I couldn't answer. Do dreams such as that one reveal an intuitive awareness of what the future will be? I could only tell her that her brother's dream death had occurred in the hatred section, and therefore was something she hated.

The rest of that dream had no other such mysteries. The dreamer loved full moons, probably because she liked to go walking in the woods at night and their light aided her in doing so. Garbage cans had an undesirable connotation to her.

Here is an important point to remember. A dream won't necessarily contain a death wish just because it shows in the love or desire section the death of someone who's alive. As an example of this, a woman dreamed the following at the beginning of a dream:

My ex-boyfriend came to the door. He was begging and pleading with me to be his girlfriend again. I didn't like the shirt he was wearing so I shot him three times: in the chest, leg, and stomach.

It may seem as if the dream was influencing the woman to love shooting her ex-boyfriend. She shot him because she didn't like his shirt, though. That is the stuff of which fantasies are made, and she undoubtedly loved only the fantasy of shooting him. Why did she love even that? She reported that while they had been going together he sometimes had worn outrageously colorful shirts. Furthermore, after they had broken up he had appeared at her door, acting as shown in the dream. She had felt pity for him--and strong feelings of annoyance as well. The violence toward him in the dream was a harmless outlet for that annoyance.

Q. Sometimes I dream about sex all through a dream. How is that explainable in terms of the dream pattern?

The sex in the first half of dreams will be with a suitable partner and will display actions your inner self approves of; the sex in the last half of dreams will be just the opposite. Incidentally, you may find some of the bad sex in your dreams to be ridiculous rather than shameful or disgusting.

For example, a woman reported that during one period in her life a number of her dreams showed her making love to King Kong. (She dreamed this mostly at the end of her dreams, but sometimes in the late-middle location.) You might wonder why she dreamed about this fictional character in that sexual context. One reason was that she didn't have a lover, and also didn't know anyone she realistically could imagine in that role. Consequently, her sexual dreams found it easier to work with fantasy than to show reflections of possible reality.

Q. Is it worthwhile to pay close attention to dreams if they're going to include silly content like that?

Dreams which superficially might seem silly can have important implications. For instance, a girl dreamed this in the first half of her dream:

Michael Jackson was a good friend of mine. I was visiting him and his family. We were going to have dinner. I was helping them set the table and they thought it was great. Later I was talking to Angie (my best friend). She said something about Michael Jackson and I said, "He's a good friend of mine." Next I was walking with some other friends of mine and a strong wind came up. I said I would fly home, and as quickly as that I was being lifted higher and higher in the air. I was trying to hold my dress down because it kept puffing out and I didn't want them to see up my dress. I looked back at them and they were standing there with their mouths open in disbelief. It was effortless for me. I put my arms out and felt propelled by the wind.

That dream could be called a silly one, and it nevertheless shows tendencies within the dreamer which perhaps are at the core of her personality. She typically may love being with people who are successful and popular (such as celebrities). And although she can't actually fly, she consistently may desire having special qualities which can impress her friends.

Her dream, in fact, also seems to contain an important clue about how the mind becomes creative. The words spoken by the dreamer indicate her conscious belief that Michael Jackson is her friend. (She may have written to him and received a reply.) Her dream was imaginative while disregarding reality's probabilities, and perhaps it may be that having optimistic, happy beliefs can boost one's imagination, regardless of how realistic those beliefs are.

Q. Do dreams reflect the dreamer's emotional health?

They can provide much information about whether the dreamer is emotionally healthy or not. We now shall examine some dreams from that perspective to find out what conclusions are possible.

A woman dreamed the following:

I am with Amy (a close friend). We are eating a meal in a restaurant with a jovial atmosphere: much chatter, high spirits, and good food. Two men unsuccessfully try to pick us up. I approach the cashier with Amy, but then realize I've left my Visa card at home. Amy takes care of my check. We leave the restaurant, and there are hordes of well-dressed people milling around outside. I see Mike, someone I'd known in high school, and his family. They are quite wealthy. Mike's father makes some complimentary comments about my hair's length and golden color. I meet Mike. He doesn't remember me, but that doesn't matter. We chat for a while in a friendly manner. I pass on out to the busy city street, and I notice I've gone ahead of Amy. I don't see her. I don't remember where we've parked the car. I return to the restaurant to find Amy. She's in the bar getting drunk. The lighting is dim and there are disreputable-looking people there.

Her dream emotions depict her as being sociable and normal. She would love eating dinner with her friend in a jovial atmosphere. It would add to the fun if two men tried unsuccessfully to pick them up. She would love it if she didn't have to pay for her meal. It would be desirable for her to meet a high school acquaintance and his rich family, and become friends with them. She likes compliments about herself when she meets people. The dream also reveals that it would be desirable if the man she had known in high school did not remember her; evidently she would want him to have an image of her different from the way she'd been in high school.

It would be undesirable to become separated from her friend and not remember where the car was. She would hate seeing her friend become drunk, especially in risky circumstances. These last dream pattern messages confirm the impression of normalcy.

The sentiments in this next example are unhappy and ambivalent. A few weeks after breaking up with her boyfriend (named Jim), a woman dreamed in the love section:

I feel extremely angry and hurt. I am packing my things to leave Jim. I am separating and folding T-shirts, sorting his from mine, and it is

hard to do because I keep getting them mixed up and have to untangle them again. He has just told me reproachfully that we don't make love any longer. Of course I would like to touch him and make love with him, but I know we can't unless we both want to. I am so upset about what he has just said.

The woman would love feeling disturbed about a relationship with Jim that hasn't yet ended. She would feel some inclination to leave that relationship, but nevertheless would love not being able to leave him easily (as would be the case if she couldn't separate their shirts). She also loves feeling upset about the fact they don't make love any longer. Clearly, she misses him despite the emotional stresses involved while they were together.

Here is a dream which indicated a state of extreme depression. A woman dreamed:

I am waiting in line with my mother to die. There is a death machine at the front of the line. Our numbers are up. The procedure is that one steps in a coffin-like box which is moving on a conveyor belt. No one is supposed to survive. The process is fast and painless. I have a difficult time saying goodbye to my mother. I don't feel ready to die. I get in the box, go underground, and everything stops. I am not killed. Instead, I come to the surface alive and I am thrilled.

At the time, the woman loved waiting to die. It would have been desirable for the dying process to be fast and painless. Not feeling ready to die would have been undesirable. She would have hated feeling thrilled about being alive.

Why did she have those emotions? She had been raped by her father and older brother, and was still experiencing the trauma of it. The dream indicates she felt love toward her mother, since they were together in the love section, but that love wasn't a barrier to feeling suicidal.

A year after that dream, she had this one:

I get raped by a man and I end up killing him because there was no other way to protect myself. I use a shotgun. Afterwards, I am

terrified about having the gun. I end up leaving the country for fear of getting found out and prosecuted.

She had evolved from being depressed to being willing to kill anyone who raped her, and she would hate feeling afraid of the consequences of that violence.

A few months later, she had this next dream:

My older brother was after me. I feared for my life. He told me he was going to punish me so I ran away. I found a woman friend I could trust. I explained to her my situation. She said it was sexual abuse. She tried to protect me but was unsuccessful and ended up giving me some herbs and wishing me well. I asked that she send someone to rescue me. I was terrified.

She loved running away from her brother. An implication is that she felt she could successfully escape from him, as otherwise she wouldn't have dreamed about that conflict with him in her dream's beginning. She desired a helpful, understanding woman friend. The image of that friend spoke for her inner self in wishing her well. Consciously (as reflected by her words at the end of her dream), she wanted someone to rescue her. Her inner self didn't assess her situation as being perilous, however, since it classified a feeling of terror as something she should hate. Overall, she felt residual conscious anxiety but also felt hope, so her mental state had improved considerably from her earlier depression.

What are our dreams like when we don't have such problems to cope with? A popular, happy woman dreamed this in the love and desire sections of a dream:

I was maid of honor at a wedding. I didn't know the couple getting married but I was chosen to be in the wedding ceremony because I fit into a long, green, sexy dress.

Look at the positive reflections in this next example. A woman dreamed in the desire section:

I had wings and they were tucked under my shirt. There were some other beings like myself that had wings and we flew to this big house where some men were. We all were women and we were charming and seducing those men. They were under our spell. I was so beautiful that people kept staring at me. I picked one of the men up and I was flying around with him. I started making love with him in the air and it was sheer and pure pleasure.

The flying leads to the lovemaking, and so the wings that are "tucked under her shirt" presumably are symbols for her breasts. The related message of that desire plot is that the dreamer enjoys lovemaking with men who find her (and her breasts) sexually attractive. The plot also shows that she isn't jealous of other women, and instead likes being part of a group of women who can collectively "cast spells" on men. The overall picture is of a woman who not only enjoys making love but also is sociable, popular, and self-confident.

Q. How else do dreams help us cope with life other than by showing our emotional health?

Many dreams provide important guidance.

Sometimes the guidance is about everyday topics, as is illustrated in the following dream. A woman who had been having problems establishing a positive relationship with her stepdaughter, Jennifer, dreamed:

I went shopping with Jennifer at a fancy department store. We stayed together as we shopped. Jennifer began bitching and begging. I ignored her.

The dream was indicating the dreamer should go shopping with Jennifer, since it was appropriate to love doing so. Staying with Jennifer as they shopped would be a desirable form of togetherness. It would be undesirable if Jennifer began the behaviors of "bitching and begging," and the dreamer should not ignore her if that happened, since she would hate doing so. The implication instead is that she should listen closely to what Jennifer had to say, and have a good talk with her.

The guidance in some dreams that are about fantasy situations may not be readily apparent, but don't stop looking for it.

A woman dreamed this in the first half of a dream:

I walked over a hill and saw thousands and thousands of bears. It was wall-to-wall brown fur. In the distance there were more bears. It seemed like they were hiding from something--that they were in some kind of danger. They were friendly and weren't menacing, even though I felt wary of them. Somebody started shooting at them and I knew I had to protect them somehow.

Perhaps that fantasy shows more than the woman's love of bears and her wish to keep them from coming to harm: the woman might feel similarly about protecting nature even if bears aren't directly involved. A tentative conclusion is that if she were to become a volunteer in environmental causes she would acquire a sense of fulfillment as a consequence.

Much of the guidance in dreams is emotional in nature, showing what to feel or what not to feel. This occurs partly because inner emotions need open expression, and the conscious self usually has to cooperate in that process, if only by not putting up any barriers against it.

A woman dreamed this in the nondesire section:

Someone who was vaguely familiar was grieving for an infant, but was displaying superficial pathos rather than the true emotion.

The implied message was that she felt unresolved inner grief which she should try to experience consciously. (She was poised and matter-of-fact when she told me that dream, but as I explained it to her she began wiping at her eyes. She then said that she'd recently had an abortion. That was what the inner sadness was about.)

The dream which follows contained emotional guidance for me. It modeled for me what I should love.

I was staying at a hotel (in real life, before I had the dream). The people on both sides were noisy, especially at night. I asked at the front desk if there was another room I could switch to, and was given a new room that not only was in a quieter wing but also overlooked a flower garden. I much preferred that new location, and as a consequence expected I would see it in the love section of one of my future dreams. Subsequently, though, I dreamed in a love section not of the new room's quietness or of the flower garden, but instead about my request to change rooms. My inner self loved the initiative I had displayed in trying to improve an unpleasant situation.

The guidance in dreams can be more explicit than that, of course. For example, a woman dreamed:

I began talking to a church congregation and started crying. I was telling the people about having fallen down a flight of stairs and killing the child I was carrying. There was a feeling inside me that perhaps I shouldn't be telling this. As I talked I felt sympathy coming from the audience. One woman was crying. Then a voice came to me. It was speaking only to me and was heard only by me. It was my dead mother. She said, "You are only doing this to create sympathy for yourself. Stop it!"

The woman loved talking about the tragedy of losing her child, and she loved being emotional about it. She had a tendency to go overboard in doing so, however, and her inner self was reacting to that. It was giving her the desire to have some reservations about speaking of the loss, and also was causing her to feel it would be undesirable to elicit so much sympathy that a listener would start crying. The dream ended by communicating inner anger toward her, and it did so via a lecture from her mother's image. The dreamer still was responsive to such lectures, even though she was a grown woman.

Some people might wonder if they should ignore dreams that show someone being angry. It's best to know about the anger, though, understand why it exists, and realize how you need to change in order to resolve it. Otherwise that anger might persist within you for a long time, accompanied by all the symptoms of depression and conflict that some professionals label as "neurosis."

The reflections in dreams about the quality of the dreamer's emotions can be like a mirror. The guidance in dreams can be like a window.

Q. Earlier it was stated that if a situation in the nondesire section actually happens, the dreamer will become impotent or frigid. Is there any sure way to avoid this?

You can try to resolve the undesirable situation in some satisfactory manner. Sometimes that's simple to do, especially when it involves something that you've done wrong. Did you neglect an important task? That can be remedied. Did you treat someone unfairly? Apologize, and do whatever else seems necessary in that person's behalf. Do you have a silly or incorrect attitude? Eliminate it. Did you act undesirably in a situation you can no longer change? Promise yourself you will never act that way again. In general, the appropriate constructive action can dispel the inner nondesire.

My dog had a deep cut on her leg, and I thought the cut would heal on its own. That night, however, I dreamed in a nondesire section of not taking the dog to the vet. It was undesirable to my inner self that I wasn't planning on obtaining medical care for my dog, and if I had continued to have that neglectful attitude I would have been impotent in any lovemaking I attempted. The inner nondesire I would have felt would have competed with and overruled the sexual arousal. (After I awoke from that dream I decided to take the dog for treatment the following day--and immediately felt sympathy for her and also was upset about my conscious stupidity. Those emotions surfaced after I'd abandoned my incorrect attitude.)

If the undesirable situation has been caused by your sexual partner, you must explain what is undesirable to you and ask him or her to change.

A woman had a boyfriend who chewed tobacco. One night she dreamed in a nondesire section that he had a wad of tobacco in his mouth as he made love to her. Since even worrying about that possibility coming true could diminish her ardor, it was necessary for her to tell him it would be undesirable to her--that chewing tobacco and lovemaking didn't mix.

What if the undesirable situation is one you can't change? Tell someone how you feel about it. You might be able to dissipate your inner nondesire in that way.

A woman was working at an institution for severely retarded, physically disabled children. One morning her supervisor told her about all the mistakes she was making. That afternoon she danced for the children during their music hour (and a few of them smiled, although most only stared with blank faces). That night she dreamed in a nondesire section that her dancing was being criticized. Her inner self wasn't trying to warn her that could happen, but instead was using that image to show she worked in an overly critical environment. The supervisor's criticism could cause her to become involuntarily frigid, and so an appropriate course of action was to express her feelings openly and fully about each occasion in which the supervisor had been critical of her. Her lover might necessarily have to be a patient listener.

Q. By understanding my dreams, will I have enough insights to avoid ever becoming impotent or frigid for psychological reasons?

Unfortunately, no. That sexual malfunctioning can be a result of anything undesirable which happens, regardless of whether it's previously been dreamed about in the nondesire section. Then, of course, if one doesn't know what's causing the impotence or frigidity one could find it difficult to resolve the underlying problem. Some people have been impotent or frigid for years because of this lack of appropriate problem solving.

That won't be your fate if you ever become impotent or frigid because of an unknown psychological cause, since you now know where to look in your dreams to find the answer. The nondesire section in a dream you'd soon have--quite possibly your very next one--would show you what the undesirable situation was. Then you could plan and carry out constructive steps in relation to it, and your sexual functioning would no longer be affected by it.

Q. I had an aunt who would become depressed at times and not know why. Could she have learned from her dreams what was causing her depression?

Yes. Our dreams inform us what causes such upsets. Here is an example of that valuable feedback, taken from the dream of a potentially snobbish and supercilious person: myself. One evening I began thinking about several people who easily could become friends of mine, and then I mysteriously felt depressed. That night the nondesire section in one of my dreams showed me not wanting some Pepsi and hamburger that were available to me, and the hatred section contained a reference to the negative mood I'd felt. These two dream sections were providing related information, and I realized what the problem was. While thinking about those potential friends, I semi-consciously had adopted the attitude that they were too ordinary and I wouldn't benefit from socializing with them. That attitude was a mistaken one. The nondesire plot was showing me that those people were sources of love, even though that love symbolically could be thought of as being Pepsi and hamburger rather than as more exotic "food." Naturally, I became depressed after deciding I didn't want to be with them.

As noted, on a conscious level I had scarcely been aware that I had formed my aloof, unsociable attitude. Such conscious ignorance might seem strange, but actually it is by no means an atypical phenomenon. The conscious self often is blind to what goes on within it. Fortunately, dreams correct that deficient awareness by pointing out what one's conscious nature truly is. It is valuable to see those reflections even when they aren't flattering or pretty.

This is the dream a woman had during a period of depression in which she occasionally thought about taking a lethal overdose of sleeping pills:

I was riding on top of a stagecoach, and men on horses were chasing it. Were they good guys or robbers? This wasn't clear to me. They drew closer and one of them shot me. Everything was black and I knew I would die.

Her dream revealed disturbances which may have been major contributors to her depression. It showed her uncertainty about men's roles, and her anxiety as well that a man would hurt her. We also see that the dream was doing its best to keep her from attempting suicide: the ending was causing her to hate the harm that could come from an overdose of pills. That constructive nature is utterly typical of dreams.

Q. Will my inner self ever give up on me? Will it ever decide I'm incapable of changing for the better, and therefore not bother putting any further guidance and support in my dreams?

No. Your dreams will always have messages designed to help you.

CHAPTER 10

DREAM INTERPRETATION EXERCISES

This chapter contains some dreams for you to analyze. See how easy--or intricate and challenging--dream interpretation can be. Pretend you have to explain each one to the person who dreamt it. What would you say in each instance? There is space available if you want to write out your analyses. The answers follow.

I purposely haven't identified dream pattern sections by name in the exercises, and leave it to you to remember that the beginning of dreams is the love section, the early-middle location shows what is desired, the late-middle plot contains what is undesirable, and dreams end with what is hated. Also, you'll have the opportunity to apply what some of what you've learned by now regarding dream complications.

1. A man dreamed this:

I was swimming. I was flowing through the water and it was almost like flying. After I finally stopped, I began having a conversation with one of the lifeguards. She was friendly and extremely beautiful. Then I found myself at work. The boss came over and started an argument with me. The argument got worse and I was fired.

Your interpretation:

Dream pattern interpretation: "You love swimming, especially when it feels as if you're flying through the water. It's desirable to talk with a friendly, beautiful lifeguard. It would be undesirable if your boss started an argument with you. You'd hate being fired."

2. A woman in the army was receiving combat instruction that required her to have training fights with other women. She didn't look forward to those fights, and one night she dreamed in the early-middle part of her dream:

Another woman and I were supposed to be fighting and I told my opponent I didn't want to hurt her and if she felt the same way we could just fake it.

Your interpretation:

Dream pattern interpretation: "Although that fake fight isn't something the army would approve of, it is desirable to you. So you may feel the urge to propose it to an opponent. Don't worry that doing so would be immoral.

By placing that fake fighting in your desire section, your inner self is indicating that it isn't morally wrong for you."

"I thought dreams contained communications from the higher self," the woman said to me.

"They do," I replied, "and your higher self would rather have you only pretend to fight than end up bruised."

She chuckled.

3. A man dreamed in the late-middle section of a dream:

A woman I met had gobs of makeup on her face. I wouldn't communicate with her.

Your interpretation:

Dream pattern interpretation: "You don't like it when women wear too much makeup, but you apparently have the tendency not to communicate such dislikes to your women companions. Your dream is trying to get you to change by defining that lack of communication as undesirable. If you think a female friend of yours is wearing too much makeup, be able to tell her that."

4. A woman dreamed this in the beginning of a dream:

I was carrying eight-month-old Alice with me as I walked through the house. Big, fat, sticky baby, she was ready for her bath.

Your interpretation:

Dream pattern interpretation: "You love carrying babies about, even when they need a bath. In general, you love raising children and being with them. They don't have to be perfect for you to love them."

The dreamer laughed as if she'd heard something ridiculous. "Of course little babies don't have to be perfect. Who ever said they did? 'Perfect!'" Her voice was indignant and maternal.

5. An 18-year-old man was given a new sports car. That night he dreamed at the end of a dream that he was driving fast on a curving mountain road.

Your interpretation:

Dream pattern interpretation: "Your inner self is concerned that you will drive too quickly on mountain roads. Even though you may have excellent reflexes, driving in the mountains is often difficult, and a mistake can prove fatal. So you inwardly would hate that fast driving. The best policy in the mountains may be to drive at what seems an excessively slow

speed whenever the road curves. Remember that it is your own inner self
that is concerned and wants you to drive cautiously."

He made a face at me.

6. A woman dreamed at the beginning of a dream:

**My boyfriend and I were at some type of gathering with a number of
other people. It seemed like a theatre at first but then it turned into a
campfire scene and then I saw the ocean. We were sitting around the
campfire and the people around us kept changing.**

Your interpretation:

Dream pattern interpretation: "You love being with your boyfriend in
settings in which other people are also present, including at a theatre,
around a campfire, and at the ocean. You typically like to be with a lot of
different people rather than with just a few familiar friends. One guesses
you're not a shy person."

She smiled. "In seventh grade I used to ask ugly boys to dance. My
karma since then is that I'm never shy."

7. A teenaged boy dreamed this:

**I was at a circus. Someone dared me to smoke some pot and then
climb one of the circus poles, which I did. While I was climbing down
I was uncoordinated and almost fell. When I got to the ground, I saw
that my niece and nephew were somehow suffering or having worse
lives because of what I'd done.**

Your interpretation:

Dream pattern interpretation: "You love being at a circus. It's desirable to you to be dared to do adventurous things, including smoking marijuana. Climbing the circus pole might be a symbol for getting high. But the rest of the dream shows some negative feelings about marijuana, and perhaps the dream is indicating you'd rather get high in a literal sense by climbing that circus pole. It would be undesirable to be uncoordinated as a consequence of the marijuana's effect, and you'd hate it if your niece and nephew suffered harm as a result of any involvement of yours with drugs. In summary, do you think your inner self wants you to smoke marijuana?"

He avoided looking at me. "I don't know," he mumbled.

8. A woman dreamed in the last half of a dream:

I started to become upset with my sister for not doing much work around the place. The argument got worse and I ended up hysterical and screaming at her.

Your interpretation:

Dream pattern interpretation: "You'd dread losing your temper with your sister. You'd hate to scream at her as your image did in the dream. If that happened in real life you'd feel dismal afterwards."

"So it's not something I want?" she asked. "A therapist told me we wish for everything that occurs in dreams."

I may have shuddered. "That's incorrect," I told her. "Those wishes only appear in the first half of dreams."

9. A schoolteacher was treated in a harsh, unfair manner by her supervisor during a staff meeting after lunch. She responded by crying, and was told she could take the rest of the afternoon off. Instead, she remained at work, and the afternoon classes with the children proceeded well. That night she dreamed in the first half of a dream of going shopping and then of meeting her boyfriend, and in that dream's late-middle section dreamed this:

I look at my watch and realize I have missed the entire afternoon of school. I feel really bad. I feel so guilty, since I am not one to shirk my duty, and here I have done that.

Your interpretation:

Dream pattern interpretation: "Your dream starts off with normal, positive experiences. You'd love to go shopping, and you'd desire meeting your boyfriend. Then the plot adds a problem which could have resulted from you taking the afternoon off and having fun. The implied message is that what happened at the staff meeting should no longer bother you, since at an inner level you prefer focusing on the entirely different problem situation shown in the dream. Your dream was being creative in depicting that alternative, preferred misery. It also was implying you should feel good about not 'shirking your duty,' since your negative feeling in the plot was opposite to how you felt about staying at work during the afternoon. Overall, the dream was trying to help you recover from the incident with your supervisor and get back to normal."

10. After her mother had died, a woman dreamed this at the beginning of a dream:

My father had died and my mother was still alive. I was with her in the kitchen at the farm. I was attempting to console her. Somehow I was at peace with her.

Your interpretation:

Dream pattern interpretation: "The dream was indicating you'd love the fantasy in which your father had died instead of your mother, and you could console her about his death. You probably have positive memories about being with her in the kitchen at the farm. Overall, though, your relationship with your mother was not serene, although you would have loved for it to be so. The feeling in the dream of being at peace with her is opposite to what you felt while she was alive."

A feeling of relief crossed the dreamer's face, and she visibly relaxed. "Dreams are curious things," she said. "It's like they can read your mind." Indeed.

11. A man lived in the city and had been forced to take his dog to the pound because the neighbors complained about it. Subsequently he dreamed in the early-middle part of a dream that a dog talked about a house outside of town.

Your interpretation:

Dream pattern interpretation: "You want to have a dog, and so you desire living in the countryside because the dog wouldn't upset neighbors there. But the fact it was the dog who spoke about the country house suggests you have repressed that desire, since your own image couldn't express that wish. Do you consciously want to remain in the city? If so, your inner self doesn't share that attitude."

12. A man dreamed at the end of a dream that an unfamiliar man swore at him in an angry voice. "You goddamned motherfucker!" that figure said, looking directly at him.

Your interpretation:

Dream pattern interpretation: "If that dream figure were someone you knew, the words might be depicting him in a role you'd hate for him to display in real life. Or if that figure didn't seem to be personally aware of you, his words might simply be something you would hate to hear. But since the speaker was unfamiliar to you and also was speaking directly to you, he evidently was an inner-self figure conveying your own inner anger toward you. Is there an important situation in your life you recently have failed to adapt to? If so, that failure presumably was unnecessary. Can you improve the situation?"

He nodded, looking grim.

13. During a snowy winter, a woman dreamed this in the first half of a dream:

I'm in a train with Darlene, my dead daughter. It's a small, old train like I used to ride to boarding school in when I was a child in England. I see sunshine and green meadows outside. Then the train stops and I go out to get a snow shovel. Darlene tells me I've left my warm woolen socks on the train.

Your interpretation:

Dream pattern interpretation: "This begins as a happy fantasy. You'd love being with your daughter on one of those old trains you used to ride in as a child. Presumably, being on those trains was a carefree time for you, and as a fantasy experience such a train ride becomes even better if your daughter is present. In contrast to the snowy conditions in your real world, you'd prefer sunshine and green meadows. But leaving the train to get a snow shovel is stepping outside the fantasy to adapt to reality; evidently you need to shovel away some snow, and the dream is being practical in reminding you of that. Then when Darlene tells you you've left your warm socks on the train, she's become a benevolent fairy godmother figure cautioning you to take care of yourself by dressing warmly. Also, you wouldn't like leaving any possessions behind on a train."

14. A woman whose son had been killed in an accident dreamed at the beginning of a dream that he said to her, "Look at my nice headstone, mom."

Your interpretation:

Dream pattern interpretation: "The image of your son is trying to cheer you up. Note that he spoke to you in the love section of your dream. Either his spirit or some inner part of you feels love toward you, and wants you to have a reason to feel happy."

She responded just as one might expect. She cried.

15. A woman who had been providing nursing care to her husband after he had a stroke dreamed at the end of a dream that she hit him.

Your interpretation:

Dream pattern interpretation: "It certainly must be frustrating at times to take care of your invalid husband. Perhaps you should consider having someone help you with him. Can you afford a part-time nurse? The fact that you dreamed about hitting him suggests you have had that impulse. Naturally, your inner self is concerned. It is causing you to hate that behavior, and in that way is trying to prevent you from hitting him even when you feel especially frustrated."

16. A youth dreamed in the late-middle part of a dream:

I was dancing with a foxy lady, but was too shy to flirt with her.

Your interpretation:

Dream pattern interpretation: "You are probably too shy with women at times, and that shyness is undesirable to an inner part of you. So start flirting with foxy women!"

17. A man who was a fan of the original Star Trek television series dreamed at the beginning of a dream:

I am on board the starship Enterprise. Aliens are attacking. They are firing their weapons at the Enterprise from short range. We can see them on the screen. They are about to break through and enter the Enterprise's control room. They will annihilate all life on board. Captain Kirk is barely able to keep them out. Explosions rip the sides of the Enterprise. How is this scene going to be resolved in the space of a one hour TV series?

Your interpretation:

Dream pattern interpretation: "You love watching suspenseful Star Trek episodes and wondering how the perilous situations will be resolved. But there's more to the interpretation. The dream shows you aboard the Enterprise, and this indicates you'd love being a crewmember on a spaceship."

"Oh, I already knew that," the man said.

18. A woman who had been physically abused as a child took karate lessons. She then dreamed at the end of a dream:

My karate instructor said to me, "You don't have to be afraid any longer."

Your interpretation:

Dream pattern interpretation: "You apparently have a lingering fear from childhood that you will be physically abused, but that fear is irrational now. No one will abuse you any longer. Your karate skills help ensure that. That is why your inner self chose the image of your karate instructor to reassure you. The fact that the dream figure spoke those reassuring words at the end of your dream indicates that your inner self would hate for you to continue being afraid."

19. A man dreamed at the beginning of a dream that he was driving along an unfamiliar road to go to a party where he wouldn't know anyone. On the previous evening, he had driven on familiar roads to attend a party where only people whom he knew well would be present.

Your interpretation:

Dream pattern interpretation: "Your plot is revealing you would love changes in your life. You would love having new places to go to and new people to meet. Many of your current experiences may be boring or lack novelty, and your dream is responding with that solution."

20. A young woman dreamed this:

It was a gorgeous sunny day. I was at my house. Suddenly these giant, fuzzy teddy bears driving red VW bugs appeared. They roared around the property, chasing me, and I finally climbed this medium-sized cottonwood tree in the back yard to get away from them. It didn't work. The biggest teddy bear drove his car right up the tree after me.

Your interpretation:

Dream pattern interpretation: "You love being at home on nice days. The teddy bears are symbols of men who are potential dating partners. You like it when they drive red VWs, and you tend to think of those men as cute and cuddly. You wouldn't want them to act so masculinely aggressive, however, that you would have to take some extreme action to escape from them. Nor is that the worst of your anxieties about men: you would hate it if a man continued to pursue you despite your attempts to escape him."

21. A man reported he had dreamed as a child:

Elves and fairies lived in the cellar of my house, and my brothers and I climbed down the ladder to play with them. Then my brothers went back upstairs and pulled up the ladder with them, and I was there alone. There was a gingerbread man stirring a big pot, and he was going to throw me in it.

Your interpretation:

Dream pattern interpretation: "You loved imagining there were actual elves and fairies. You liked playing in the cellar with your brothers, and it would have been nice to play with those imaginary beings as well. You wouldn't have liked being abandoned in the cellar. As for the scary dream ending--

"Was there a man you were afraid of when you were a child? The gingerbread man may be symbolizing an actual person, and if so the dream is reflecting a fear involving him."

"My father and I never got along," the dreamer said. "He used to beat me."

22. A youth had pizza with some friends. During the meal he tried to impress the girl sitting across from him by telling her how he had helped his uncle break horses at his uncle's ranch. He made some exaggerated statements about working with the horses, and wondered if she truly believed him. That night he dreamed in the early-middle plot of a dream that he gave her a slice of pizza, and she smiled at him.

Your interpretation:

Dream pattern interpretation: "You want the girl to enjoy being with you, and giving her the pizza was a symbolic wish for that. She did not respond to your conversation as you had hoped, though. Her smile in the dream was opposite to how she actually felt. Yet it's certainly possible that she could like you and enjoy your company, since otherwise you probably wouldn't have had that wishful dream about her. Try to find the right ways to relate to her."

23. A man worked with a woman who was friendly, attractive, and efficient. She was happily married and had two small children. One night he dreamed at the beginning of a dream that he was in a wedding ceremony getting married to her.

Your interpretation:

Dream pattern interpretation: "You'd love it if you could marry her, but that is an impossible goal. The dream is showing a happy fantasy, and at the same time is implying that you'd love marrying someone like her."

24. A young woman dreamed in the early-middle part of a dream:

My younger sister visited me at college. She wanted to play soccer, so we rode our bikes around looking for a game. We found one, but they were practicing for a match and wouldn't let us play. We decided to go shopping, and ended up in a lingerie department. A scummy old man kept looking at us to make sure we didn't steal anything.

Your interpretation:

Dream pattern interpretation: "That plot is showing various desires of yours. You'd like for your sister to visit you at school. No doubt her visit would be a welcome change for you from doing homework. It would allow you, for instance, to ride your bike around looking for a soccer game. But the soccer players in the dream didn't let you join their game, and that implies you would rather end up going shopping with your sister than playing soccer with her.

"You like shopping for lingerie, but the plot seems to indicate you've felt tempted in the past to steal such clothing items. It's desirable to your inner self that you resist that temptation, and that is why it created the male figure who watched you closely. That man was your conscience, in a sense, and he appeared scummy because your inner self felt some anger toward you and accordingly wanted your dream to become unpleasant at that point. If you were to begin stealing items from stores that inner anger would intensify, and you might find yourself having nightmares."

25. A woman reported that as a child she had dreamed at the end of a dream that clowns were crying at a grave. Questioning brought forth the information that during that childhood period her older sister frequently acted like a clown, and as a consequence received a lot of attention from others.

Your interpretation:

Dream pattern interpretation: "The clowns at the grave were crying about the death of a fellow clown: your sister. The fact that you dreamed about her death in your dream's hatred section reveals you would have hated for her to die. But why did your dream find it necessary to include that mourning for her death? You undoubtedly felt jealous of her when she received attention from others for her clowning, and you may even have wished--at a conscious level--that she were dead. Your inner self didn't want you to feel that way, and therefore caused you to see the clowns crying.

"That crying is opposite to what an inner part of you actually felt about your sister's playful, extroverted behavior. It was hard for you to enjoy that behavior consciously, though. That is why inner-self figures cried in the dream, rather than your own image."

* * * * * * * * * * *

How did you do on this quiz? Don't feel bad if you were unable to interpret all of the examples. Some of them--the last, especially--may have proven difficult for you. Yet that difficulty is only a reflection of inexperience, and will soon vanish as you interpret more dreams.

CHAPTER 11

REMEMBERING DREAM MESSAGES

Most dreams, when we're trying to remember them, seem as flimsy and insubstantial as cotton candy at the fair (although that's not truly an appropriate comparison). Yet their messages are of such potential importance that not being able to remember them could be a great loss.

To remember dreams, some people train themselves to awaken fully at night in order to write their dreams down (or speak them into a recorder), and compile dream diaries to refer to ever afterwards. One woman showed me a collection of her dreams which she'd bound in leather, and the title on it in big red letters was **Visits From The Dream Faerie**.

All that isn't necessary. While half-awake, still lying in bed with your eyes closed, it's easy to analyze what you remember of a dream, note its messages, and store them away in your memory for future recall. You don't have to remember the overwhelming mass of details, but only those underlying messages. That greatly simplifies things.

The first step, of course, is to be able to remember at least some of the dream plot well enough to analyze it. Here are two exercises to carry out before falling asleep which can help you become more aware of your dreams and better able to remember them subsequently.

(1) Try to see images and colors in your mind's eye as vividly as you can. It doesn't matter what you see but rather that you have the opportunity to see various imagery in natural ways. Hopefully, when you start this procedure in relaxed, drowsy conditions, your mind will cooperate by producing spontaneous images. Don't try to force any of it to become what

you consciously want it to be; that might make it and future imagery go away. Instead, focus on seeing each image as it actually is, even if this means allowing it to be vague or blurred rather than specific. Proceed in this manner for a minute or two.

You'll probably see your dreams better that night, and as a consequence remember them better.

(2) Count your thoughts as you spontaneously think them, and once you've counted five try to remember what each was. If you can, focus as well on how you thought each one, assuming there were any noticeable thinking sensations which accompanied the thoughts. Repeat this same procedure with one or two new sets of thoughts.

This is a memory tune-up, and its effects can help you remember dreams without any conscious effort on your part.

Even if these two exercises prove beneficial, you may find upon awakening from a dream that you can only remember some of it. That's all right. You can still analyze that part, providing you can identify in which dream section or sections it appeared. And with the dream fresh in your mind, that identification process may occur naturally and immediately as you try to do it.

The next step is to analyze the dream material. Will this be hard to do? Perish the thought! Based on what you've now learned about dream interpretation, few, if any, of your dreams will require prolonged efforts to understand.

Let's see how this nighttime analysis might occur in practice, using the following example. A woman experiencing some troubled relationships remembered dreaming this in the early-middle part of a dream:

I had gotten away from some situation I needed to escape from, but I wasn't totally out of danger. Some people were after me and I didn't want them to catch me. I went into a groovy hair salon and went up to a woman with wild hair and said "I need help." She thought I was talking about my hair, and said "You sure do." She started throwing blue paint and something else on my hair. I was aware of the people I

wanted to escape from in back of me but it seemed as if they couldn't get me because I was around another person.
Next I was watching a television commercial being made for some perfume. There was an incredibly gorgeous man and a beautiful woman in it, and they seemed to be making up the script as the commercial continued. The man was a jerk because he was very promiscuous, just playing with all his different women. Suddenly, I was in the commercial. I was dressed in a beautiful red satin dress and my hair was done up in a fancy way. Some music started and the man came over to me. We also made up a script as we talked. It was about seduction.

The interpretation begins by identifying that plot as showing desires of hers, since she dreamed it in the early-middle section of her dream. The subsequent analysis would proceed as follows (using some educated guesses). She desires that she escape pursuit, and since she can do that by being with someone, perhaps the "escape" is from her own loneliness rather than from people who want to continue distressing relationships with her. She expresses a need for help to a hairdresser who then mistreats her hair. This semi-revengeful outcome suggests her inner self has been irritated about the past appearance of her hair, which may have been as wild as that of the hairdresser's. The plot then shows a man and woman in a symbolic perfume commercial which allows them to be spontaneous with each other; the dreamer evidently desires such spontaneity in her conversations when she talks with a handsome, flirtatious man. She also desires a promiscuous man, and she would like to appear attractive to him.

These conclusions are readily apparent and can be made in a drowsy state. Nor would the dreamer need to write down that dream to preserve her memory of it. Instead, she need only make these "shorthand" notes to herself: wish to be with someone comforting or safe; hairstyle irritation; want spontaneity with handsome, seductive man who plays around; want to be as attractive as possible.

Such brief, clear messages tend to stay with us the following morning, even after the alarm clock rings and the day competes for our attention.

CHAPTER 12

PROMISES

You will be able to analyze the true meanings in your dreams. Those messages from your inner self often will be surprising, and some of them may contradict your conscious views. But you will see that dreams contain the brilliance and compassion to help you get back on the right tracks when you consciously go astray. At times you may be amazed by the ability of your dreams to get in touch with reality, including its more unusual aspects. Some of your dreams may seem to have telepathic communications. Others may feature starring roles for wise, loving fairy godmothers. Undoubtedly, a number of your dreams will reflect down-to-earth topics and interests. All of your dreams can prove valuable to you.

You will know how to interpret even extraordinarily complicated dream plots, and many of your dreams will be instantly clear in meaning to you.

All of this begins tonight.